THE CIVIL WAR IN THE NEW RIVE

New River Valley
Modern Roads, Days 1, 2 & 3

Map 2

Contents

Theater Maps of the New River Valley, 1861-1864 . . . . . Inside cover and page 1

Day One — 1861

Introduction 4
Geography of the Region 5
List of Stops 5
Chronology of Day One Driving Tour Events 6
Historic Map of Day One Driving Tour Area 7
Modern Roads Map of Day One Driving Tour Area 8

Day Two — 1862-1863

Historic Map of Day Two Driving Tour Area 36
Modern Roads Map of Day Two Driving Tour Area 37
Overview 38
List of Stops 39
Chronology of Day Two Driving Tour Events 40

Day Three — 1862-1864

Introduction 83
Historic Map of Day Three Driving Tour Area 84
Modern Roads Map of Day Three Driving Tour Area 85
Geography of the Region 86
List of Stops 87
Chronology of Day Three Driving Tour Events 88

Acknowledgments 142

THE CIVIL WAR IN THE NEW RIVER VALLEY 3

Listing of Maps

Distances are not to scale unless otherwise indicated.
On the maps, **bold** numbers within circles indicate Tour Stops.
Names, units, and placement that are in blue are Union; those in red are Confederate.

Day One

Map	Description	Page
1	Historical Theater	Inside cover
2	Modern Roads	1
3	Day One Historical	7
4	Day One Modern Roads	8
5	Kanawha Falls to Hawks Nest, Oct. - Nov. 1861	13

Map	Description	Page
6	Cotton Mountain – Artillery	15
7	Kanawha Falls – Stop #4	18
8	Kessler's Cross Lanes	20
9	Carnifex Ferry Battle	22
10	Spy Rock to Sewell Mountain	28
11	Battle of Fayetteville	31

Day Two

Map	Description	Page
12	Day Two Historical	36
13	Day Two Modern Roads	37
14	Area of Raids	43
15	Powell's Raid	45
16	Peter's Mountain Raid	48
17	Tuckwiller Hill	50
18	Battle of Lewisburg	53
19	Averell's Route to White Sulphur Springs, 1863	61
20	Battle of White Sulphur Springs	63

Map	Description	Page
21	Webster's Raid, Huttonsville to Huntersville	66
22	Battle of Huntersville	67
23	Averell's Second Raid	70
24	Droop Mountain State Park	72
25	Droop Mountain Battle	73
26	Approaches to Droop Mountain	74
27	Averell's Third Raid (Salem Raid)	81

Day Three

Map	Description	Page
28	Day Three Historical	84
29	Day Three Modern Roads	85
30	Union Advance on Clark House	91
31	Driving Map of Modern Princeton, W.Va.	94
32	Movements, May 1862	95
33	Battle of Princeton "Pigeon Roost"	99
34	Battle of Giles Courthouse	102
35	Averell's and Crook's Routes, May 1864	105

Map	Description	Page
36	Preliminaries to the Battle of Cloyd's Mountain	106
37	Battle of Cloyd's Mountain (double map)	109
38	Cove Mountain Battle (double map)	119
39	Toland's Route, July 1863	122
40	Toland's Raid at Wytheville	126
41	Saltville Area	130
42	First Battle of Saltville	133
43	Burbridge's Route over Clinch Mountain	141

The Struggle for the New River Valley

The New River Valley was a minor but significant theater in the Civil War. The New River Valley posed strategic and tactical problems for both the Union and Confederate forces which played a vital role in the logistical warfare that eventually determined the military outcome of the Civil War. Nearly every military event in the New River Valley has been written about by local historians. Yet, as a theater of operations, the New River Valley has been almost totally overlooked: not a single work has ever been done on the whole area.

At the outset of the War, no political boundary separated the parts of Virginia. The military and political leaders of the War saw the New River as a single entity. In both 1861 and 1862, Confederates launched offensive operations to secure the lower New River and Kanawha River valleys that contained vital strategic materials, salt, lead and communications links. As these offensives were blunted, the Confederates went over to the defensive, trying to protect strategic assets at the southern (upper) end of the Valley. Confederates would continue to raid north into the Valley.

The Union forces, after stemming the Confederate offensives, began their own offensive operations that lasted more than three years before successfully attaining their objectives in the southern end of the Valley: the railroad bridge over the New River at Central Depot (Radford), the lead works near Wytheville, and the salt works at Saltville. To succeed, the Union forces had to learn a new way of warfare–the long distance raid. The Union success in the New River Valley played a vital role in the defeat of the Confederacy.

In **1861** the struggle between the forces established Union control over the Kanawha Valley and Gauley Bridge. Confederates dominated the rest of the theater–a line that ran from Flat Top Mountain to Sewell Mountain to Droop Mountain.

In **1862** both sides attempted traditional combined arms (infantry, artillery, and cavalry) offensives to break the line. These attempts failed, largely due to logistic and terrain problems.

In **1863** both sides turned to **raids,** trying to find the right formula for this theater. In **1864** and **1865** the Federal forces mastered the raid strategy and accomplished their objectives.

During the four years of war in the New River Valley, there was a distinctive pattern of concentration and dispersion of forces linked to the seasons and needs of the major theaters of the War. In the New River Valley, major operations took place in the spring and fall. In the summer both sides usually made substantial troop withdrawals to reinforce the major campaigns in both East and West. During the summer months, the theater was torn apart by skirmishes between partisans, guerilla irregulars, and small regular units left behind to hold the lines. In winter, the theater was largely used as forage by troops from both sides in preparation for a spring offensive.

Geography of the New River

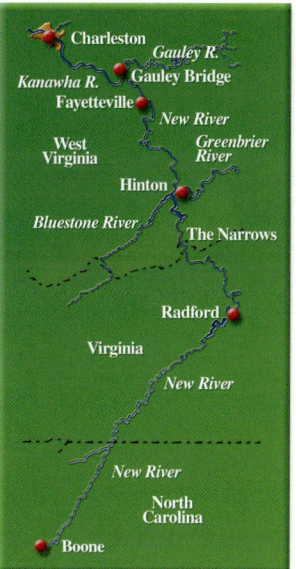

The New River begins in the mountains of western North Carolina, flows some 250 miles going northeast into western Virginia, then turns northwest through "The Narrows" into West Virginia. After entering West Virginia, the River pushes through the Allegheny Mountains, carving out the 65-mile New River Gorge from Hinton to Gauley Bridge. At the northern end of the Gorge, the New River is joined by the Gauley River, forming the Kanawha River, which flows another 90 miles west to the Ohio River. The river was discovered in the 1670s by English explorers seeking furs and a passage to the Western Ocean. While named the New River, geologists suggest that it is, ironically, one of the oldest rivers in North America. The river was flowing northwest before the uplift of the Appalachian Mountains, creating the Gorge. The Gorge at the northern (lower) end of the River narrows as the river passes through the mountains. At the southern (upper) end, the River passes through the open valley in Virginia. All of the New River Valley provided difficult terrain for all the military operations of the Civil War.

Overview of Day One

The Day One Tour takes you to the sites where Union and Confederate forces met in 1861 to gain control over the New River Valley and its valuable strategic assets. The tour guide describes the travel routes to the nine sites of the first day tour. Maps and narratives in the Tour Guide will explain both events leading to the sites as well as what to look for at each site. Page one of the guide contains a general overview of the New River campaigns. The guide contains maps showing both the modern roads used on the Day One Tour and the historic road network of 1861. The guide also has maps showing the tour and historic routes for all three days of the Tour.

There are **nine** stops on the first day tour:
Stop #1 The Visitors Center of the New River Gorge National Park–an introduction to the terrain of the New River Valley theater of the Civil War
Stop #2 Hawks Nest State Park Overlook–a view of the Gorge
Stop #3 Gauley Bridge–lower end of the New River, and an introduction to the battles for control of the New River Valley
Stop #4 Falls of the Kanawha–the end of "steam" transportation supply lines
Stop #5 Kessler's Cross Lanes–the "Battle of the Knives & Forks"
Stop #6 Carnifex Ferry State Park–the site of the Battle of Carnifex Ferry
Stop #7 Spy Rock–the advance of forces to Sewell Mountain
Stop #8 Sewell Mountain–the area of confrontation between Lee and Rosecrans
Stop #9 Fayetteville–the "Battle of Fayetteville"

Chronology for First Day Tour

The "Stops" on the tour do not follow in chronological order; that would require a large amount of doubling back and zigzags. As you tour, you may refer to the following chronology.

July 1861 Confederate forces holding the Kanawha Valley are attacked by Union forces and fall back into the New River Valley.
August 1861 Union positions are established from Gauley Bridge to Summersville.
August 26, 1861 Confederate flanking movement, engagement at Kessler's Cross Lanes.
September 10, 1861 Union forces attack at Carnifex Ferry.
October 1861 Confederates retreat to Spy Rock and Sewell Mountain. Union forces advance, then pull back.
November 1861 Confederates attack on Gauley Bridge from Cotton Mountain. Union forces counterattack and advance to Fayetteville.
May 1862 Union offensive advances toward Princeton and Lewisburg (Day Two Tour), then retreats to Flat Top, Fayetteville, Hawks Nest.
September 10, 1862 Confederates take the offensive. Battle of Fayetteville. Confederates occupy the Kanawha Valley.
November 1862 Confederates retreat from Kanawha Valley, back to upper New River.
May 1863 The last Confederate attack on Fayetteville uses "indirect fire."

The tours begin at the Visitors Center at **Tamarack,** located at exit 45 on the West Virginia Turnpike-Interstate 77/64, in Beckley, West Virginia. The Day One Tour is approximately 155 miles in length, and returns to Tamarack.

Instructions will indicate the distance between turns and stops. The symbol (**TM – 00**) will indicate the total miles traveled to that point. In most cases mileage will be "rounded off" to the nearest mile. Odometers may vary considerably so the mileage indicated may not match yours, but by carefully following directions and using the maps, you should not get very lost. Don't hesitate to ask local residents for directions. The tours can best be done with a companion reading directions. **You should read all the directions in each travel section before starting that section, because the directions also contain things to look for as you go between "Stops."** At each "Stop" read the information and then explore the area as suggested. Be respectful of private property at some "Stops."

Both in the text and on maps, names, units, and placements that are blue are Union, those in red are Confederate.

Start the tour by proceeding **North on Interstate 77, traveling 2.3 miles to Exit 48. At Exit 48 go north on Route 19.** There is a $.25 toll to leave the interstate. **Go north on Route 19 for 20 miles to the turn for the "Visitors Center of the New River Gorge National Park"** (TM – 23). Note that Route 16 joins and leaves Route 19 several times between Beckley and Fayetteville. Make note at TM – 21 of Route 16 – You will be returning to this turn after **Stop #1.**
—Turn right off Route 19 and park at the Visitors Center —— Stop #1.

THE CIVIL WAR IN THE NEW RIVER VALLEY 7

8 THE CIVIL WAR IN THE NEW RIVER VALLEY

Map 4

Day One
Modern Roads

Stop #1 – Visitors Center–Canyon Rim–New River Gorge National Park.

The Visitors Center is open daily except Thanksgiving, Christmas, and New Year's Day. When you enter the Visitors Center, take note on the left wall of the aerial photograph of the area. Also note the horizontal contour map of the New River Valley. Notice how this steep gorge divides the two flanks of the valley. This division had a direct impact on military movements. Note the road network on both sides (Northeast and Southwest). The gorge was a significant military barrier. Once either Union or Confederate forces were committed to the roads on one side of the gorge, it was difficult to move to the other bank. As each side planned offensive or defensive troop movements between 1861-1862, they had to guess where their opponents would commit their troops.

Military operations in the Civil War period were dependent on massive supplies being provided by steam propelled transportation, the railroad and steamboat. Therefore, most Civil War campaigns were fought along railroad lines and navigable rivers. The New River Valley had neither of these. The Kanawha River was navigable by steamboat from the Ohio River to the Falls of the Kanawha (Stop #4) just before the beginning of the New River Gorge. No railroads led to, or through, the New River Valley in the upper (North) end. At the southern end of the Valley, the Virginia Central and Tennessee Railroad, from Richmond to Memphis, connected to Covington, Va., on the southeast end of the valley and to Wytheville on the southwest end of the Valley. The James & Kanawha Turnpike linked the span between the Kanawha Falls and Covington, while the Fayette-Raleigh-Grayson Turnpike linked the span between the Kanawha Falls and Wytheville. (See Map 1.) Both these roads were more than 120 miles of horse drawn wagon transportation. An offensive operation along either road presented almost insurmountable problems for both sides. Control of the road network was a key issue throughout the war.

As you drive any of the three Day Tours, you will have an opportunity to appreciate not only the beauty of the New River Valley but the difficulties that both sides faced in this rugged terrain. Don't miss the spectacular view of the New River Gorge from the Visitors Center. You may want to take the short walk to the Overlooks of both the River and the Bridge.

Leaving the Visitors Center, return to Route 19. **Turn left on Route 19 (south). Cross back over the New River Gorge Bridge, go 2 miles to the junction with Route 16** (at the traffic light). **Turn right on Route 16 North toward Gauley Bridge. Drive 7 miles on Route 16 to the junction with Route 60.**

As you drive this portion of the tour, you will descend into the New River Gorge along Locust Creek, cross the river, and ascend the north side of the Gorge to Chimney Corners. The first 4 miles of this route follows the path of the old Fayette-Raleigh Turnpike and was the main road toward Charleston and the Kanawha Valley. The hamlet of **Beckwith** was the site of camps for troops on both sides that were trying to block the road. Just past **Beckwith** a road (Deepwater Rd.) turns left. This is the old turnpike, the main road, that passed to the south of **Cotton Hill,** then on to the Falls of the Kanawha. CR–13 is not passable to current traffic. The present day road, which winds down to the bottom of the Gorge, was a small dirt track in 1861. At the bottom of the Gorge, cross the new bridge. From the bridge, if you look right, upstream of the New River, Hawks Nest is just around the bend in the River. To the left, the river flows toward Gauley Bridge.

> **Proceed to the intersection with Route 60 at Chimney Corners (TM – 34). Turn right (east) on Route 60. Go 2.5 miles to Hawks Nest Overlook. Park at the Overlook Parking Lot on the right side of the road. Walk the loop path (about 200 yards) to the Overlook. The path starts near the center of the Parking Lot and returns to the east end of the parking area.**

Across the road from the parking area is a gift store, snack bar, and restrooms open from April-October, 10:30 a.m. to 5:00 p.m.

Stop #2 – Hawks Nest Overlook – part of the West Virginia State Park at Hawks Nest. The rest of the Park is 1/4 mile further east on Route 60.

Route 60 follows the bed of the James & Kanawha Turnpike, the major road on the northeast side of the New River Gorge. Hawks Nest was a well known tourist stop in the early 19th century, having first been called "Marshall's Pillar" because Chief Justice John Marshall, in 1812, had measured the distance from the river up to the rock ledge. While no major military action took place at Hawks Nest, the spot was regularly visited by troops passing by on the nearby turnpike. The road was easily blocked in this vicinity, and several minor skirmishes took place nearby. As you stand at the Overlook, you might want to imagine an incident that happened on October 12, 1861. When the Confederates retreated from Gauley Bridge toward Lewisburg, they sent a supply train and some 32 captured Union prisoners, escorted by 12 Confederate soldiers. As they approached Hawks Nest, the Federal prisoners asked to be allowed to take a look at the 650-foot drop. The rebels hesitantly agreed, put the prisoners in front, and formed a semicircle near the edge. The Corporal of the Guard became concerned that the huddled prisoners might be hatching a plot to rush the outnumbered guards and throw them over the side. He ordered the guards to "fix bayonets!" The shocked prisoners then believed they were about to be pushed over the side. Some tense moments! They all were relieved to get "away from that place."

THE CIVIL WAR IN THE NEW RIVER VALLEY

In the 1930s, another event at Hawks Nest had a much worse ending. In order to drill a hole through the mountain so the river flow could produce hydroelectric power, several thousand miners were set to work just below the Nest.

The problem was that the mountain was composed of almost pure silica. The drilling produced a deadly silicone dust that the miners breathed and therefore began to die. Several hundred died, a monumental tragedy which was covered up at first. Then investigations led to needed changes in safety laws. In the New River Valley, beauty and danger are never far apart.

> Leaving the Hawks Nest Overlook—**turn left on Route 60, going west, back in the direction you arrived from. Go west on Route 60 for 7.5 miles to Gauley Bridge.** After passing Chimney Corner, you may want to pull over at the Hawks Nest Golf State Park (TM-41).

At this location stood the plantation home of Confederate Colonel Christopher Tompkins, commander of the 22nd Va. Infantry. Tompkins' home, "Gauley Mount," was the finest in the area, consisting of a "palatial house . . . well-kept lawn, barns, stables, and slave quarters."

When General Rosecrans' Union troops occupied the area, he used this site as his headquarters. Confederate Col. Christopher Q. Tompkins assumed field command of the 22nd Va. Inf. in 1861. His wife, Ellen Wilkins Tompkins, and their children stayed at the estate at Gauley Mount (about three miles east of Gauley Bridge). The estate had fallen into Union hands when the Rebel army retreated.

Col. Tompkins wrote directly to Generals Cox and Rosecrans, asking for protection for his family and property. They established a "gentleman's agreement," and the Union forces treated the family very well. When it became apparent that the Confederates would not retain control of the area, the family returned to Richmond with "a wagonmaster supervising a carriage, two four-horse-drawn wagons, a cart of furniture, and Ellen Tompkins with two sons, three female slaves and their five children, two puppies, and two chickens." That must have been some sight going east on the Turnpike.

After the Sewell Mountain confrontation (stop #9) Col. Tompkins, disgusted with the squabbling of Generals Wise and Floyd, and fearful for his family, resigned his command and went to Richmond, where he spent the War working at the Tredegar Iron Works. In 1861 it was still a "gentleman's" war. The house survived the War but was later burned.

THE CIVIL WAR IN THE NEW RIVER VALLEY

> **As you approach Gauley Bridge (TM-44) look for the "Gauley Bridge Visitors Center–Tourist Information Center" sign just before the bridge. Park at the Visitors Center. –Stop #3–** The Visitors Center is a Gift Shop. **Walk to the left of, then behind, the Gift shop (by the Veteran's Memorial under the tourist sign), and go a few steps to the right. You can see the Gauley River as it joins the New River, forming the Kanawha River. Notice the stone piles beside the modern railroad bridge. These piles are from the original bridge burned in 1861. Back across the road from the Visitors Center, on the New River side, is a "Scenic View" with a small shelter over a bench, 100 yards to the left. Go to the bench.** From the bench, you can see Cotton Mountain directly across the river, and the rest of the features described at **Stop #3**.

**Stop #3 –Gauley Bridge –
July 1861-November 1862
—An overview of the Campaign.—**
(The commentary at Stop #3 is extensive, giving you an overview of the events at the lower end of the New River preparing you for the rest of the tour.)

At the outset of the Civil War, the counties south of the Kanawha River in southwestern Virginia had indicated support for the Confederate cause and had endorsed the Resolution calling for the secession of Virginia. In June of 1861, Union forces under the command of General George McClellan occupied the counties of northwest Virginia that had remained loyal to the Union. In May, a movement had begun to create a new state. In the Kanawha Valley, sentiment was divided between Union and Confederacy. By July of 1861, pro-Confederate militia had formed into units loyal to the Confederacy. Under the leadership of General Henry Wise, the Confederates had taken control of Charleston and the Kanawha Valley. On July 17, 1861, Union forces under the command of General Jacob Cox invaded the Kanawha Valley but were temporarily blocked at the battle at Scary Creek just west of Charleston. On July 24, having learned of McClellan's victory further north at Rich Mountain, Wise, fearful of being cut off in the Kanawha Valley, began a "retrograde movement" toward Gauley Bridge. The struggle for the New River Valley had begun.

General Wise decided to fall back east toward Lewisburg on the James & Kanawha Turnpike. As he passed through Gauley Bridge on July 26, he ordered the destruction of the bridge that spanned the Gauley River. When Cox's force arrived on July 29, they began to realize the difficulties of pushing on into the New River Valley. Cox sent scouts east along the James & Kanawha Turnpike, and established a base at Gauley Bridge that could be supported by steamboat as far as the Falls. (Stop #4). General Wise was joined at White Sulphur Springs by General John Floyd and his Legion. Both generals were former governors of Virginia, and longtime political rivals. Floyd argued for offensive action to regain the Kanawha Valley. Wise argued for defensive action to draw the Federals into the southeast end of the New River Valley where they would have to fight at the far end of a supply line. By mid-August, Floyd, disgusted with Wise's inaction, seized the initiative and advanced toward Gauley

THE CIVIL WAR IN THE NEW RIVER VALLEY 13

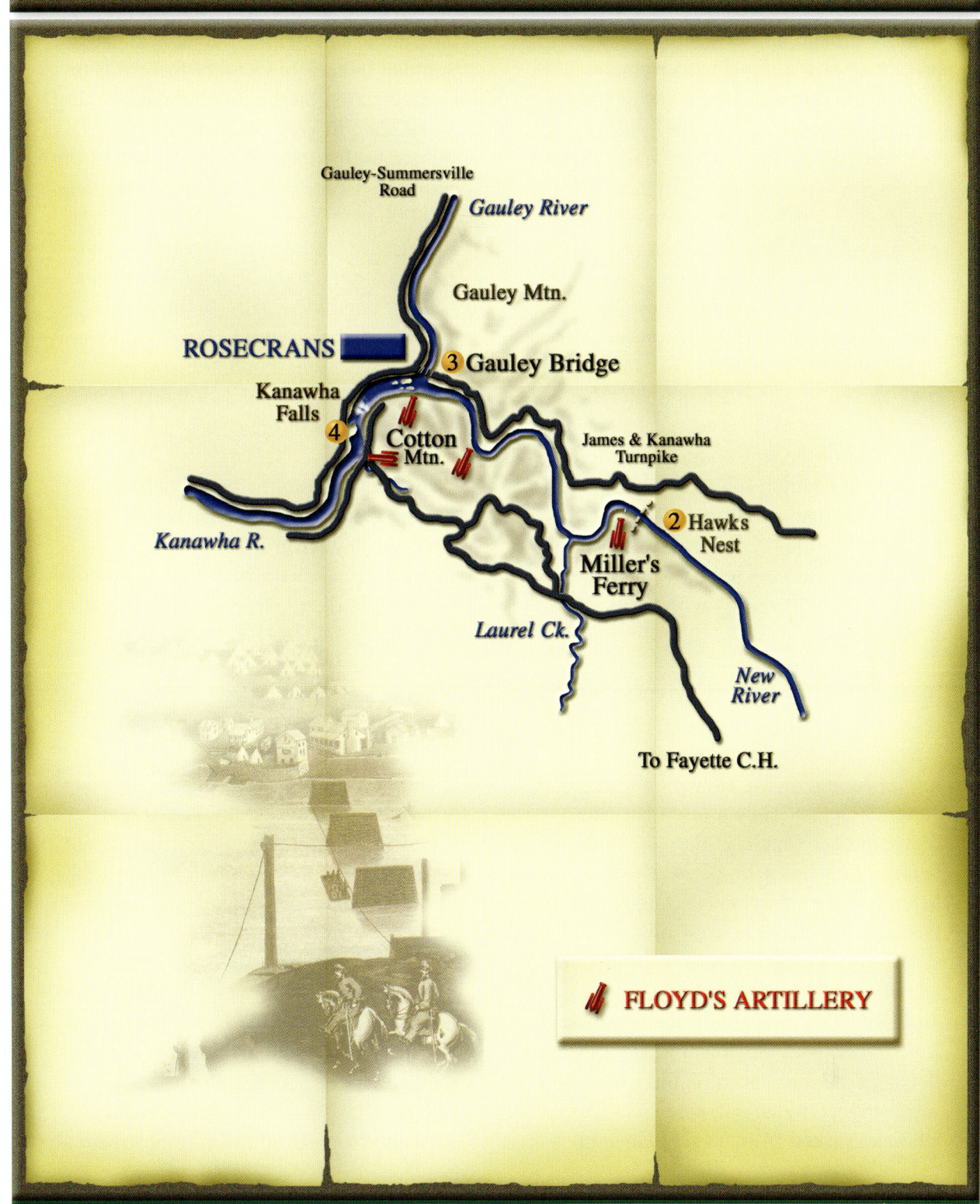

Bridge, hoping Wise would advance and provide support.

Cox, aware of the possibility of a Confederate advance, had placed troops near Hawks Nest. He also sent the 7th Ohio Regiment up the Gauley River to protect against a flanking movement, and to maintain communications with Union forces north at Summersville. Floyd attempted the flanking movement to the Gauley River, resulting in the battles at Kessler's Cross Lanes (Stop #5), and Carnifex Ferry (Stop #6) in late August and September. Meanwhile, Wise had slowly advanced toward Gauley Bridge. The Confederate defeat at Carnifex Ferry caused the retreat of both Wise and Floyd back to Sewell Mountain in September. General Robert E. Lee was sent to take command of the squabbling Confederates and face the Union forces under General Rosecrans that had advanced to Sewell Mountain (Stop #8). After weeks of rain, Rosecrans and Cox fell back to Gauley Bridge in October 1861 with more than 5,000 men.

In the fall of 1861, while Cox was digging in at Gauley Bridge, he reported the following incident. Lieut. Wagner ordered the 2nd Kentucky Inf. to work one night on entrenchments. They refused because they had been on picket duty the night before. Sergeant Joyce – 2nd Ky. Inf. told his men not to obey. Lieut. Gibbs, the District Commissary, drew his pistol and said, "That's mutiny. Order your men to take the tools or I'll shoot you." Joyce said, "Shoot." Gibbs did. Joyce fell dead. Joyce's company ran to get their rifles and threatened to kill Gibbs on the spot. They were stopped by an unarmed Gen. Cox who had rushed from his tent when he heard the commotion. Lt. Gibbs stood trial and was acquitted because of the mutiny.

In October, Floyd resumed his aggressive movement. He not only wanted to disrupt the Union supply line, but he also had a political intent. In October there was to be an election on the issue of establishing a new state in Western Virginia. Floyd wanted to disrupt "the first election of the counterfeit state of Kanawha." With nearly 4,000 men, he crossed the New River, advanced from Fayetteville, and placed artillery on the top of Cotton Mountain without being detected. In the early morning fog, on Nov. 1, 1861, Floyd began a weeklong bombardment of Gauley Bridge as well as infantry fire from the banks of the river.

(See Map 5. From the bench at Stop #3 Cotton Mountain is directly across the river; Gauley River is to the right rear. Kanawha Falls is downstream around the bend of the river; Miller's Ferry is upstream.)

The artillery fire was frightening, but not effective. By Nov. 3, Rosecrans and Cox had learned that Lee had been recalled to Richmond and that no Confederate troops were advancing along the James & Kanawha Turnpike. Floyd's troops were all by themselves on Cotton Mountain. Rosecrans planned a four-prong encirclement to trap Floyd. General Benham, with reinforcements, was to approach from Charleston along the Turnpike, cross to the south side of the River, get behind the Confederates blocking the road to Raleigh Court House, south of Fayetteville. General Schenck was to cross the New River 15 miles upstream at

Townsend's Ferry and get to Fayetteville from the east. General McCook's Brigade was to cross at Miller's Ferry. General Cox would engage in a holding attack straight across the river from Gauley Bridge. Cox had built several boats for his amphibious assault, estimating he could put 500 men an hour across the river.

The attack was set to go on the night of Nov. 6. During the day on Nov. 6, six long-range Parrot guns had arrived, and their fire began to suppress the Confederate bombardment, causing the withdrawal of the guns. Continued rains had swollen the river; Benham cautiously decided not to move. Days passed. In frustration Cox decided to attack on Nov. 10. The 11th Ohio and 1st Kentucky pushed the Confederate skirmishers aside and climbed the steep mountain. Floyd realized his dangerous position and quickly withdrew. Benham's delay had allowed Floyd to escape. Gauley Bridge was safe for the moment. General Benham was sent to a court martial. He spent the rest of the war on engineer assignment, for which he was better suited.

In January 1862, the Union built a wire suspension bridge over the Gauley to replace the bridge destroyed in July. The bridge was a technologically advanced design, 585 feet long, 10 feet wide, with three spans held by one and a quarter inch wire cables. They weren't sure it would hold, so they marched the 28th Ohio on to it for a test. One can only imagine what these German troops thought about being used as guinea pigs.

In the spring of 1862, General Cox launched an offensive from Gauley Bridge. He sent an attack as a feint east toward Lewisburg, while the main attack went south through Fayetteville, Raleigh, on to Princeton and Giles Courthouse (See Day 2 Tour). After three battles, supply problems caused a withdrawal back to the northern end of the Valley.

In late summer 1862, Union forces were largely withdrawn from this theater to counter Lee's invasion of Maryland that resulted in the Battle of Antietam. Confederate General William Loring, aware of the Union troop withdrawal, decided to launch an offensive to regain control of the Kanawha Valley. In Sept. 1862, Loring's 5,000 Confederates attacked 1,500 Union forces at Fayetteville (Stop #9), and pushed on around Cotton Hill and Gauley Bridge. As Union forces withdrew and the Confederates moved toward Gauley Bridge, the new wire suspension bridge was destroyed. There are three different accounts of the destruction: 1) it was hit by Confederate artillery fire from Cotton Hill; 2) it was burned by retreating Yankees; 3) the suspension cables were cut. It is unlikely that Confederates would have destroyed a bridge they needed. As the Confederates moved toward Charleston, a legend began that in their haste a cannon was left behind on Cotton Mountain in a deep ravine. Even today, dedicated relic hunters still comb the Mountain for the "Lost Cannon."

The Confederates occupied Charleston and the Kanawha Valley for a month. Tons of salt and supplies were captured and sent back to the East. Loring was then ordered to march north through western Virginia to support Lee's attack. He realized the impossibility of supplying such a march and refused to comply with his orders, even planning an evacuation of the Kanawha Valley. He was relieved by General Echols, who immediately saw the difficulty of trying to sustain his position at the wrong end of the 120-mile supply line. The Confederates retreated out of the Kanawha Valley for the last time in the Civil War. By November 1862, Gauley Bridge was back in Union hands where it would remain, giving the Federals permanent control of the lower end of the New River Valley. (The railroad line that you see at Gauley Bridge was built in 1873.)

> **Leaving Stop #3, continue west on Route 60 for 4 miles, turn left into "Kanawha Falls Park–Public Fishing Area." Stop #4 at (TM – 46).** When leaving Stop #3, you will immediately cross the new bridge. At the first intersection, Route 39 will turn into the town of Gauley Bridge. **Do not turn; stay on Route 60 west.** (Make note of the turn as you will be coming back here after Stop #4.) At (TM – 45) you will pass the site of the Union ammunition dump that came under fire when the Confederates were bombarding from Cotton Mountain in Nov. 1861. Just before you reach Stop #4, you will pass the Glen Ferris Inn. (See Map #7)

Stop #4 – The Falls of the Kanawha –

From the parking area you have a spectacular view of the Falls that prevented any further steamboat navigation up the river. In 1861, water powered mills were at either end of the Falls. After parking your car, walk to the right of the parking lot, on the river side, away from the Mill that you see on the left of the Falls. Take the path for a hundred yards, to the river side looking at Cotton Mountain. The small community on the other side of the river is Kanawha Falls.

In the winters of 1862 and 1863, this was the site of Camp Reynolds, winter quarters of the 23rd Ohio, the regiment whose membership included Col. Matthew Stanley (future Supreme Court Justice), and Rutherford B. Hayes and William McKinley, both future Presidents of the United States. Further downstream was Montgomery Ferry, which provided a river crossing for the Turnpike from Fayetteville, which came south of Cotton Mountain, through a gap you can see just south of the town.

During the Confederate bombardment in November of 1861, one section of guns was on Cotton Mountain just above where the town is today. On Sept. 3, 1861, Captain Ralph Hunt –1st Kentucky Inf.— was ordered on a reconnaissance up the thickly brush covered heights across the river, overlooking the road that the Confederates might advance on. A Confederate scouting party led by Lieutenant Loughborough got behind the Yanks. At about 50 yards Loughborough raised his rifle and yelled, "Come out you damned Yankee son of a _____, and be shot!" Both officers fired at the same time. Loughborough fell dead. The Confederates rushed Hunt, capturing him and sending him to Richmond as a prisoner. He was later exchanged.

Walk back to your car.

18 THE CIVIL WAR IN THE NEW RIVER VALLEY

Map 7

Kanawha Falls / Cotton Mountain / Hawks Nest

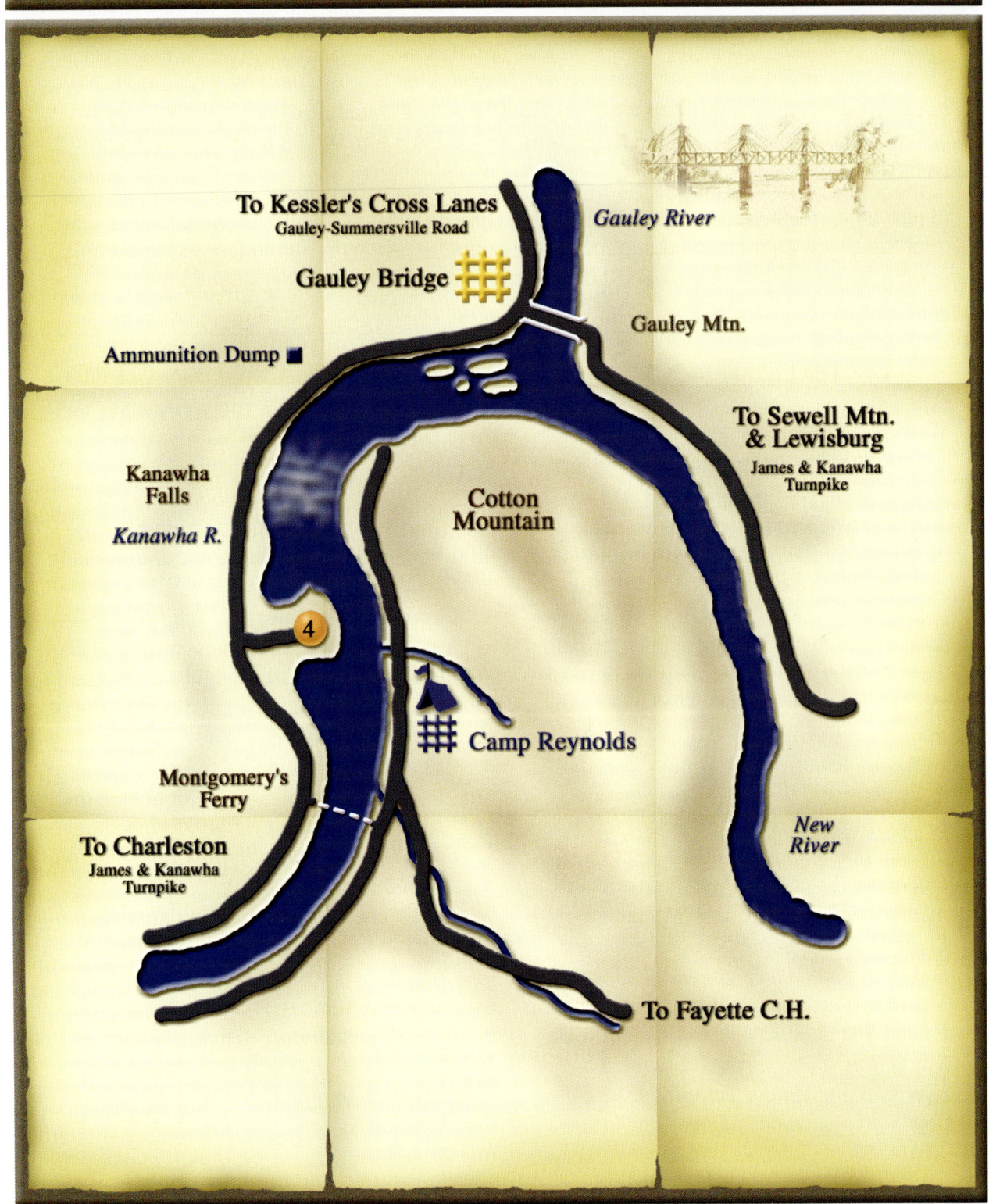

THE CIVIL WAR IN THE NEW RIVER VALLEY

> **Leaving the Falls of the Kanawha, turn right and go east on Route 60, back in the direction from which you came. Go 4 miles to the junction of Route 39 just before Gauley Bridge. Turn left onto Route 39; pass through the town of Gauley Bridge (TM-50). Go 18 miles north on Route 39. You will be driving along the Gauley River for a few miles. A little past four miles (TM-54), Route 39 will bear right, crossing the railroad tracks and through the town of Belva. At (TM-68) turn right at the Junction of Route 129. There is an Historical Marker, "North & South," at the Junction which gives information about Kessler's Cross Lanes.**
>
> **Go 4.5 miles on Route 129. You will see a sign for Kessler's Cross Lanes. SLOW DOWN. Just around the bend, 0.2 mile, turn left into the parking lot of the Zoar Baptist Church (TM-72).**

Walk up to the paved path through the cemetery. This is a short, but steep walk. Take your time. Go to the top of the paved path. You will be able to see all the battle area.(See Map 8.) Walk thirty yards to the right (north), where you will overlook the Zoar Church down to your front-right (east). You should be able to see the road running from the right by the Church, left downhill toward the Cross Lanes. You will be standing on the hill where several Companies of the 7th Ohio retreated.

Stop #5–Kessler's Cross Lanes– "The Battle of the Knives & Forks" Aug. 26, 1861

After the Battle of Rich Mountain in July, General McClellan was called to Washington and General William Rosecrans was put in charge of Union forces in western Virginia. His 9,000 men were spread from Clarksburg to Summersville along the Gauley Bridge–Weston Turnpike running north-south through central western Virginia. Rosecrans also commanded Cox's force of nearly 5,000 around Gauley Bridge. By mid-August, Generals Wise and Floyd, with Lee's encouragement, were going westward along the James & Kanawha Turnpike with a combined force of 5,000. Floyd hoped that Wise would demonstrate directly toward Gauley Bridge, while Floyd would take his force north of the Turnpike along the Sunday Road, cross the Gauley River at Carnifex Ferry, and then cut the road between Gauley Bridge and Summersville at Kessler's Cross Lanes.

Cox anticipated this move and sent the 7th Ohio with 750 men led by Col. Erastus Tyler to occupy the road junction. Tyler had been in the fur business before the war, and it was said that he "was sent to (West) Virginia to 'skin the rebels.'" He established a camp on the evening of August 25, placing Companies C and A on the hill east of Zoar Church. Another company was sent to the hill north of the Cross Lanes. The rest of his troops were camped along the road by the Church. Col. Tyler neglected to post outlying guards. At 5:00 a.m., 1,700 Confederates, 45th Va., 22nd Va., 36th Va., 50th Va., a Company of Cavalry, and three guns approached the camps.

Major Robert Glass described the Confederate movement, *"At 4 o'clock a.m., the Brigade was in motion. . . in the fresh morning air. . . . A heavy fog hung over the hills and along the valleys, and*

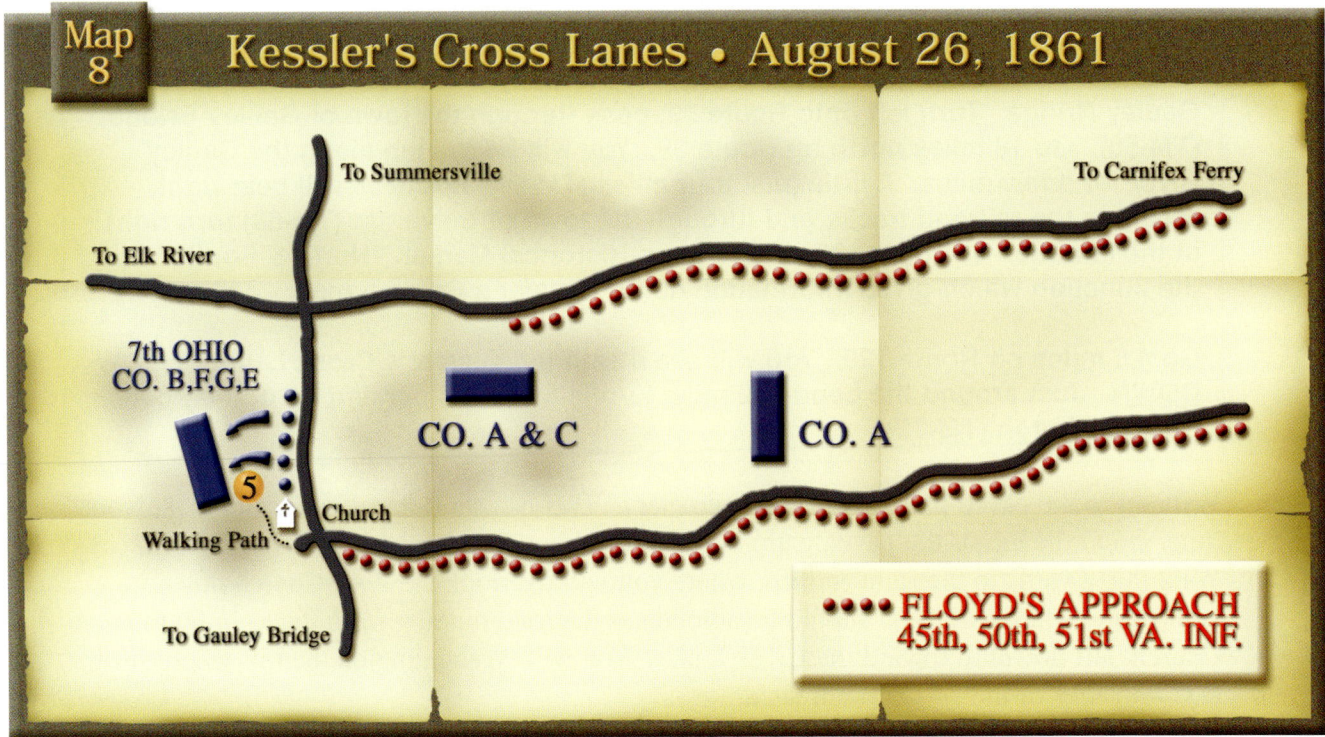

we approached almost upon the enemy's pickets before they saw us. They fired and ran. . . . Our men gave a shout . . .and dashed at accelerated speed. In a few minutes we discovered the blue coats of the enemy, as they stood drawn up near a church by the road side, while to our right and behind a fence stood another column of the enemy."

The skirmish has been called the "Battle of Knives & Forks" as the Union was surprised preparing breakfast. Companies A & C were nearly surrounded but put up a good fight, allowing the companies on the road to run up the hill west of the church and form a defense (where you are now standing).

The fighting lasted less than an hour. The Confederates seized the road and were moving toward the flanks of the hill. The pickets of Company C that were on the forward hill were a different sort of soldier. They were very religious, mostly from Oberlin College in Ohio. Their comrades taunted them, calling them the 'Praying Company," and scorned them for their continual reading, and writing their diaries. Many were skeptical of their ability to fight. At Cross Lanes they proved their mettle, putting up the best fight of the day, firing into the flanks of the Confederate column which moved on the road from Carnifex Ferry. (See Map 8.)

Private Leroy Warren–Co. C wrote, *"When the bullets first began to whistle around me, cutting the leaves and grass and ploughing up the ground, I was considerably frightened, and would have given worlds to have been somewhere else, but . . . it seemed to me that the bullets would not hit me and that they were almost harmless. I saw the First Lieutenant . . . shot in the arm; the man who stood beside me put his arms to his breast with a groan and staggered back, but I had no fear. I was only careful to get behind a stub while loading and to take as good aim as possible. Once the enemy's line was entirely concealed by smoke, I fired where the smoke seemed to be the thickest."*

The 7th Ohio decided to run for it. With the road cut, they had to scramble through the back country. Some went to the northwest, beating a path over the hills all the way to Charleston. Eventually about 600 made their way back. Company C, the "Praying Company," lost more than 40 men; Union casualties totaled about 150. The Confederate casualties were about 40.

Failure to pursue the defeated 7th and a quick move to Gauley Bridge cost Floyd a chance to move into the Kanawha Valley. Cox had wired Rosecrans for help even before the battle. Floyd began to realize that even though he had shattered the 7th Ohio, and had taken the Cross Lanes, he was way out in front and could be trapped by converging Union forces. Floyd decided to fall back three miles to his camp at Carnifex Ferry.

> **Leaving the parking lot at Zoar Church, continue north on Route 129. At the bottom of the hill 0.3 of a mile, the road bears sharply to the right–at the "Cross Lanes." Stay on Route 129 for one more mile. Look for the sign for "Carnifex Ferry" (TM-74). The sign is slightly hidden by a road sign. Go straight ahead to Carnifex Ferry. Leave Route 129 which turns sharply to the left.** (You will be returning to this intersection after a stop at Carnifex Ferry.) **Continue 1 mile until you enter Carnifex Ferry State Park. Proceed to the parking area at the Henry Patteson House (Stop #6a).** (The State Park has labeled this the Patterson house. The house belonged to Henry Patteson, according to Terry Lowry, the author of *September Blood, the Battle of Carnifex Ferry.*)

Stops #6a, 6b, and 6c –The Battle of Carnifex Ferry– September 10, 1861

When General Floyd fell back from Kessler's Cross Lanes after his victory on August 26, he did not want to abandon his foothold on the north side of the Gauley River even though he could be quickly attacked by superior forces of Rosecrans and Cox. To defend his position meant he would have the high cliffs of the Gauley and the swift river immediately at his back–a very poor military position. His easy victory at Cross Lanes made him overconfident. He chose to dig in. Maybe Wise would send help. Wise slowly moved toward Hawks Nest and ordered General Chapman's Brigade of Confederate militia to move from Raleigh (Beckley) toward Fayetteville. Not much

Patteson House

help for Floyd.
After the disaster at Kessler's Cross Lanes, Cox called for help from Rosecrans, who responded quickly. On September 9, Rosecrans had nine Ohio Regiments formed into three Brigades and

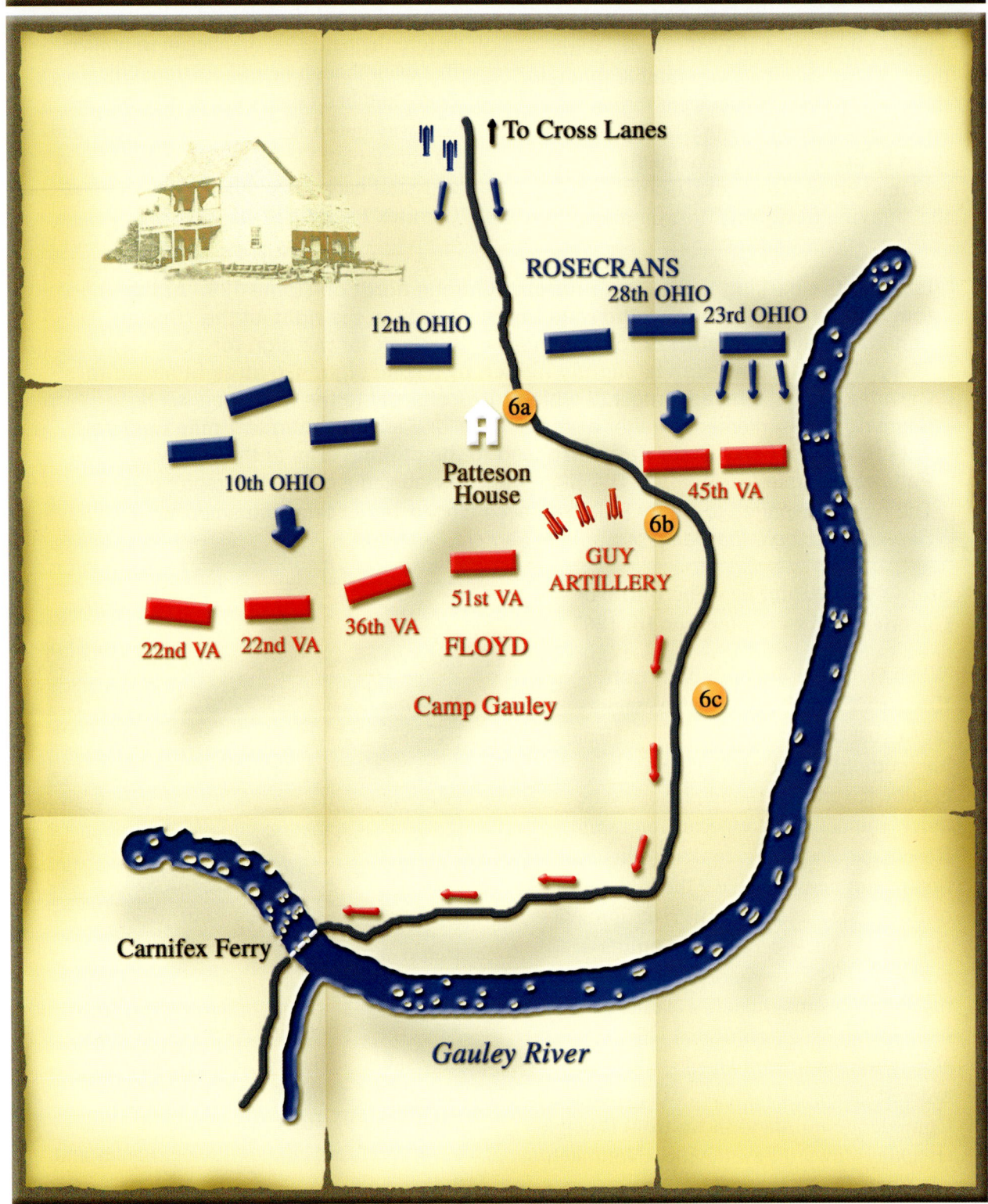

Map 9: Carnifex Ferry Battle • September 10, 1861

THE CIVIL WAR IN THE NEW RIVER VALLEY 23

several artillery units, a force of 7,000, camped 8 miles north of Summersville, about 15 miles from Floyd. The Confederates in Floyd's camp had 2,000. The force from Kessler's had been reinforced by the 51st Va., and two artillery units.

On September 10, Rosecrans approached with his column stretched out for miles. He had little knowledge of the location or strength of Floyd. Floyd had even less knowledge of Rosecrans and did not expect any Yanks to approach his camp before the 12th. Neither commander nor troops were ready for the battle. Most of the soldiers had not been under fire. This would be their first fight. The Union column was led by General Henry Benham's First Brigade of the 10th, 12th, and 13th Ohio Regiments.

At about 3:00 p.m., the lead regiment, the 10th, approached the Confederate works. (See Map 9.) The Confederate line was stretched between the cliffs of the Gauley, with the River protecting the flanks. In the center, some cut timbers protected the guns of Guy's artillery.

The 10th Ohio was deployed to the west of the Patteson House and moved on the Confederate works. The battle had begun. Two Confederate men were writing letters home when attacked; one letter was later found where pen and ink had been spilled. Another ended with the line, "To Arms. To Arms. I am called for the attack." The author, Captain Robert Snead-50th Va., survived the battle and returned to finish the letter.

You may walk 100 yards from the parking lot back to where you will see an artillery piece. The Park signs near the gun, and around the Patteson House, will help explain the fighting.

For the next three hours, Rosecrans made the mistake of sending his forces into the battle in piecemeal, as they arrived by Regiments. The Confederates easily repelled these weak attacks. Col. Lytle of the 10th Ohio was able to get his troops to within about 30 yards of the Confederate position but fell back seriously wounded. In another attack, Col. Lowe was killed as he led a charge of the 12th Ohio on the right flank. By early evening, the 23rd Ohio had worked through the woods and attacked the line of the 45th Va., finding that there wasn't any open flank. As darkness settled in after 7:00 p.m., the 23rd Ohio and 28th Ohio mistakenly fired on each other in the dark woods of Pierson Hollow.

Go back to the Parking Lot by the Patteson House. There is a path across the road from the parking lot, down into the gully, that the 23rd Ohio used to move toward the Confederate position. The path circles around behind the Confederate line coming out in the field behind the line. This is a pleasant hike that will take at least a half hour, if you have the time for a walk. After visiting the Patteson House area, drive to the Confederate line–there is no parking lot, so pull over to the side by the "farm road." Do not drive down the "farm road." (Stop #6b.)

General Floyd had positioned himself just to the rear of Guy's guns, standing on the stump of a chestnut tree cut about five feet above the ground. In the first 15 minutes of firing, Floyd was hit by a minie ball in his right arm. He was treat ed and returned to combat in about 10 minutes, encouraging his men to fight on.

Walk around the reconstructed Confederate works.–Then drive to the parking lot at the back left end of the Park. (Stop #6c.) Walk to the overlook of the steep cliffs behind the Confederate right. You are looking 450 feet down on the Gauley River, one of the premier whitewater rafting rivers in the eastern United States. Time permitting, you may use any of the several trails that go down to the river, including the old road bed to the site of Carnifex Ferry. These are long trails. Note all these trails are steep. Use caution if you take one of these trails.

Sunset brought an end to the battle on September 10. Rosecrans rejected a proposal for a night attack. The incident in Pierson Hollow had demonstrated the dangers of confusion of night fighting by "green" soldiers. His losses had been light despite the awkward charges. Artillery on both sides had, with their lack of experience, fired too high throughout the battle and caused very few casualties.

Sixteen-year-old John W. Blizzard had been sent from home to take a basket of food to his father in the 36th Va. Inf. A Rebel officer refused to let the boy leave once the battle had started. John Blizzard fought, and later it was reported that "young Blizzard fought harder and was scared worse than in any of his subsequent battles and that this battle so affected him that he aged in that afternoon to such an extent that he never afterwards felt like a boy."

The Yanks had lost 27 killed or mortally wounded, and 103 more wounded.

Rosecrans spent the night preparing for a coordinated assault the next day. Floyd was buoyed by his success. He had been lucky at Cross Lanes, and now with the ineffective attacks by a superior force, and with a slight wound, he could be satisfied. But his biggest luck was still to come.

He knew he was outnumbered and would be overrun the next day, so he decided to retreat at 10:00 p.m. One by one his regiments were pulled out of line and went down the difficult Ferry Road. A Union advance would have caught his army strung out and helpless. You can imagine the fear of the last unit down the hill – the 22nd Va., but all worries were groundless. The Yankees were asleep. Floyd escaped with none killed and only 20 some wounded.

Both sides would claim victory. The Union won the field, the Confederates the battle. Floyd joined Wise back on the James & Kanawha Turnpike where they fell back eastward to Spy Rock, then to Sewell Mountain. (Stops #7 & #8)

Aftermath of "battle"– Carnifex Ferry was the first "battle" for most of the forces involved. Many of these units would meet many times during the four years of war. In May of 1864, at the Battle of Cloyd's Mountain (Tour Day 3), 7,000 Union forces would once again fight 2,000 Confederates. At the climax of that struggle, Col. Rutherford Hayes, leading a Brigade, would send the 23rd Ohio to break the line held by the 45th Va., the same units that faced each other at Carnifex Ferry. Although Carnifex Ferry had been light in casualties, at Cloyd's Mountain the Union lost 688, the Confederates 538. The blundering, amateur soldiers of 1861 had become deadly professionals by 1864.

THE CIVIL WAR IN THE NEW RIVER VALLEY

The "Battle" at Carnifex Ferry had an important political effect. Beginning in May of 1861, meetings had been held in Wheeling to organize a "Loyal" government for western Virginia. In October 1861, just after the "victory" at Carnifex Ferry, the "Loyal Reorganized Government" submitted a proposal to create a new state to the voters, a plebiscite. The vote took place in areas controlled by Federal forces. The favorable vote was a beginning step in the formation of the new State of West Virginia. A loss at Carnifex and Confederate occupation of the Kanawha Valley might have changed that vote. Floyd's retreat was a real victory for the Union.

> **As you leave Carnifex Ferry State Park by the same road you entered the Park, the tour mileage should be (TM–76). Go back on the road you entered on for 1 mile to the junction with Route 129. Turn right. Proceed east for 5 miles to the junction with Route 19.** You will pass by Summersville Lake on the left, and go along the top of the Summersville Dam of the Gauley River, a very scenic area.
>
> **Turn right on Route 19. Go 10 miles south to the junction with Route 60.** You will pass over the Meadow River which flows into the Gauley just above Carnifex Ferry. Notice how each of these rivers has carved out steep canyons that become obstacles to military movement. **Exit from Route 19 to the right, and then turn left on Route 60. Go east toward Rainelle (TM-93).** (At this point if you want to shorten the tour, stay on Route 19, continuing south. You are only five miles north of the Visitor's Center of the New River Gorge. You will miss Stops #7 & #8).
>
> **Go east on Route 60 for 3 miles, to Spy Rock (TM–96).** On Route 60 you are back on the James & Kanawha Turnpike, only 18 miles east of Hawks Nest, and a mile east of the Sunday Road that goes to Carnifex Ferry. **SLOW DOWN as you approach Spy Rock. You will pass by the Jeanette Cemetery on the right. Go 0.1 mile. You will see a large rock. Pull off into the road on right. There is an Historical Marker–"Spy Rock."**

Note on the James River & Kanawha Turnpike

Before 1786, the route of travel west in Virginia was the old "Buffalo Trail" used by General Andrew Lewis on his march to Point Pleasant in 1774. In 1784 after urging from George Washington, the Virginia Legislature authorized the construction of a state road. In 1790 the road was completed from Lewisburg to the Falls of the Kanawha–The James River & Kanawha Turnpike. At first it was used to haul salt from the "Kanawha Salines." In 1827 a stagecoach line was established, and by 1830 the stages were running three times a week, with rest stops every 15 to 20 miles. In the 1850s cargo wagons were so numerous that as many as thirty would pass any spot in a few hours. Going east they carried salt and whiskey; going west, merchandise and tobacco. More than 60,000 hogs and cattle from Kentucky and Ohio passed along the Turnpike in any given year. One of the stage stops was at Lookout near Spy Rock.

View from Spy Rock, with Sewell Mountain visible on horizon

Stop #7 —Spy Rock— Camps—September-October, 1861

After Carnifex Ferry, General Floyd retreated south on the Sunday Road to the James & Kanawha Turnpike. He turned to the east and marched to Lookout, the village just before Spy Rock. Lookout is at the midway point between Charleston and Lewisburg—about 60 miles from each. About one half mile west of Lookout is Spy Rock, a cliff used by Indians and whites to spy on approaching enemies from the direction of Big Sewell Mountain to the east.

General Wise's force had been pushed back from Hawks Nest by Cox's advance from Gauley Bridge. The two Confederate forces continued to fall back toward Sewell Mountain, 14 miles farther east from Spy Rock. Floyd learned that two new Regiments, 13th Ga. and 14th N.C., were being sent to him and were at Meadow Bluff, 15 miles farther east. Floyd decided to move to Meadow Bluff. Now, Wise and Floyd continued to argue, but reversed their roles. Wise insisted on staying at Sewell Mountain. As Floyd moved east, Wise reportedly yelled out, "Men, who is retreating now? John B. Floyd, damn him, the bullet hit son of a bitch, he is retreating now."

September 15, Cox's men arrived in the vicinity of Spy Rock, where they could just see the top of Sewell Mountain off to the east. The Union soldiers took pleasure in "appropriating" supplies from the local tavern keeper, George Alderson, who also operated the stagecoach stop and toll gate at Spy Rock. He eventually submitted a bill to the U.S. Government for $4,664.09, but for the moment he was out of business. Local Confederate sympathizers did not fare well with the Union occupation troops.

You might climb up Spy Rock, but be careful, there is no path. The brush can be thick.

While camped near Spy Rock, a wagon master reported that there was a Confederate camp just to the south between Lookout and the New River. Scouts seemed to verify the story, and a plan was made to surround the "enemy camp." Col. Botecour was to take a Kentucky regiment around a road to get behind the camp, while Col. McCook, with an Ohio regiment, would block any escape. Botecour pushed through the thick brush and finally saw the target camp. Just as they were about to fire, they discovered the camp was filled with Union soldiers. They had gotten "turned around" (lost) in the woods and circled behind their own camp. There was no Confederate camp. Col. Botecour had a hard time living with the reputation of being a "Backwoods Guide."

From August through September, Confederates of both Wise and Floyd clashed with Cox's men in a series of ambushes and skirmishes along the Turnpike. Lt. Col. Joseph Frizzell's 11th Ohio Inf. became skilled at long range

Spy Rock

patrols and ambushes. The Regimental history of the 11th Ohio reported:

"We need more men in our little command, but as it is, we have done as much work as any regiment in Virginia, had more skirmishes, killed more rebs, and received less newspaper praise than any regiment in Virginia. We are now called 'Frizell's Gipsies,' as we are here, there, and everywhere, and when the rebs think they have us, we ain't there. They have tried to surround us three or four times, but as we generally know as much of what they are about as they do themselves, they are rather unfortunate in their efforts. . . . we have been over all their big hills, can sleep in logs, behind stumps, in rain or shine, can make the biggest show with the fewest men, and the biggest fight on record."

By September 17, General Cox had established his headquarters at Spy Rock and was calling for supplies from Gauley Bridge: "Send us some salt, vinegar, molasses . . ." General Rosecrans was sending troops forward along the Turnpike, as the Confederates were digging in at Sewell Mountain. The armies were about to face each other again.

On October 5, Rosecrans, down to only 5,200 hungry effectives, decided to pull back. October 6, Lee wanted to attack and suggested that Floyd take a force to the south side of the New River to flank Rosecrans. Col. Henry Heth of the 45th Va., an old friend of Lee, told Lee that Floyd was not capable of independent command. Back at Spy Rock, Cox, with more than 500 sick, decided to fall back to Gauley Bridge, ending the campaign. Lee, at Sewell Mountain, let the militia go home. With his losses from sickness, Lee was down to 4,000 men.

Floyd had been sent off to flank Gauley Bridge (see commentary from Stop #3). Lee expected to advance west along the Turnpike toward Gauley Bridge, but realized another 30 miles of washed out roads would result in impossible supply for his weakened force. On October 15, Lee began to pull back east to Meadow Bluff. The 14th N.C. Regiment had come to Sewell Mountain with 750 men; as they returned to Meadow Bluff, they were down to 277– all without fighting. The deadliest place in the Civil War was not the battlefield. Floyd continued to circle around toward Gauley Bridge, but Lee was called back to Richmond, ending his poor performance in western Virginia and leaving Floyd walking into a potential trap.

Sewell Mountain was left as a no-man's-land between the two armies. Drier years ahead would see the return of Union soldiers.

Leaving Sewell Mountain, return to Route 60. Turn right going west. Drive 18 miles back to the junction with Route 19 (TM-128). Turn left, going south on Route 19 toward Beckley. Drive 8 miles. Turn left at Laurel Creek Road. You will pass over the New River Bridge. **Go through the intersection with Route 16. Turn left at the Laurel Creek Road Exit off Route 19.**

THE CIVIL WAR IN THE NEW RIVER VALLEY 31

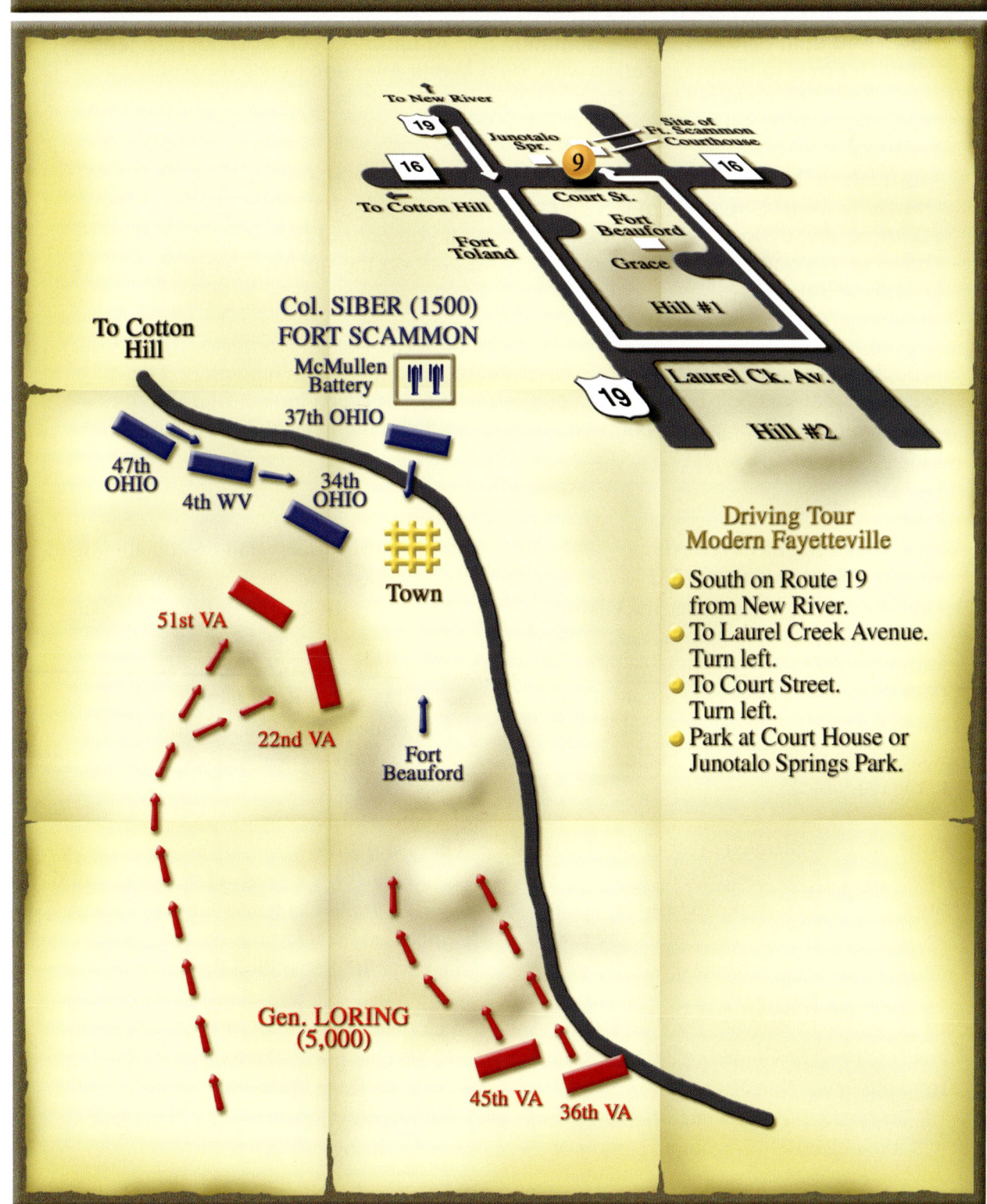

> Just past the intersection with Route 16, notice the high ground to the right of the road. This is the position of the Confederate left flank during the battle (see Map 11-Inset). A year later this hill was fortified by Union forces.
>
> **Before arriving at Laurel Creek Road, you should look at the maps of Fayetteville, the roads and troop positions. The town of Fayetteville has grown and the battlefield has been covered over by present-day homes. You will drive through the town and then park to read the commentary. At Laurel Creek Avenue, turn left; drive 1/2 mile to the intersection with West Maple Avenue.** Notice the higher ground on both sides of Laurel Creek Avenue: on the right is Hill #2, to the left Hill #1. This was open ground in 1862.
>
> **Turn left on Maple Avenue. Drive 0.7 of a mile to the traffic light at the intersection with Court Street. Turn left on Court Street. Park on the right in front of the Courthouse, by the Historical Marker signs. If you cannot find a parking place here, go a block farther on Court Street and park on the right by Janutolo Springs Park.**
>
> Maple Avenue follows the route of the Kanawha-Fayette-Raleigh Turnpike. Just after you turn on Maple, you will pass Grace Street on the left. On the high ground on Grace Street was Fort Beauford, the outlying post of the Union force. There were 1,000 yards of open ground between Fort Beauford and the main Union position at Fort Scammon.

**Stop # 9–Battle of Fayetteville–
September 10, 1862–
General Loring's Confederate Advance**

(See Map 11.) The modern town of Fayetteville has grown over all of the battlefield of 1862. Use the maps, and some imagination to envision the battle. Refer to the chronology.

After the Confederate retreat in November 1861, most of the Confederate sympathizing residents of Fayetteville had evacuated south, leaving only a few families in town among the Union occupiers.

In the fall of 1862, when the Confederates learned of Union force withdrawals from the lower New River, General Loring began a Confederate offensive with the objective of regaining control of the Kanawha Valley and coordinating with Lee's invasion of Maryland (Antietam Campaign). With 5,000 men assembled in Monroe, Giles, and Mercer counties, Loring chose to move up the southwest side of the New River using the Turnpike from Princeton, to Raleigh, to Fayetteville and then into the Kanawha.

Two Federal Regiments, the 34th & 37th Ohio, and a battery of artillery, a force of 1,500 under the command of Col. Edward Siber, were left to hold Fort Scammon which had been built in Fayetteville in January. In preparation for his advance, Loring had sent a raiding force of 550 men under Jenkins from Lewisburg, circling to the north around Charleston to block the Kanawha Valley. The Union commander, Col. Joseph Lightburn, at Gauley Bridge was aware of Loring's advance and also aware that no Confederates were approaching from the northeast along the James & Kanawha Turnpike. He ordered Col. Siber to try to hold Fayetteville and pulled the two regiments he had north of the River to Gauley Bridge where they could be sent to support Fayetteville.

By the early morning of September 10, Loring was ready to move on Fayetteville. At 5:00 a.m., four miles south of Fayetteville, a skirmish between pickets caused a deployment of the advancing Confederates. By 11:00 a.m., skirmishing more than 4 miles from town caused General Loring to send out a flanking movement westward. General John Williams, with a local guide, took the 51st and 22nd Va. Regiments on a 13-mile march to cut the Fayette-Kanawha Turnpike and threaten Fayetteville from the west (see Map 11). Loring continued up the Turnpike with his main force. A half mile south of town another Federal ambush caused Loring to deploy the 45th Va. to seize Hill #1 and Hill #2. As the Yanks at Fort Beauford resisted, the 45th worked its way through some woods to the left, as the 36th Va. advanced, taking fire from the Fort as well as the Federal artillery back at Fort Scammon. While the hard fighting was taking place, by 2:15 p.m., the Confederate flanking force had arrived, hot, tired, and thirsty, but was in place to cut the Turnpike and put the Yanks in a crossfire. Col. Siber responded to the danger on his right by sending nearly half his force, the 34th Ohio, to attack the Confederates on the flanking hill. During the late afternoon, the 34th launched three attacks, failing to take the hill but pushing the 51st back from the Turnpike. Hearing the sounds of battle, Col. Lightburn at Gauley Bridge sent elements of the 4th (West) Va. and 47th Ohio infantry, and 25 horsemen from the 2nd Va. (USA) Cavalry, toward Fayetteville. During the hot afternoon, Union water carriers made the dangerous dash to bring refreshments from Janutolo Springs to the gunners in Fort Scammon. Just after sunset, the fighting on the flank slowed down, and the 37th Ohio took the moment to launch a bayonet attack at the Confederates to their front. While this attack was underway, the Union reinforcements from Gauley Bridge began to arrive along the Turnpike. By 9:00 p.m., the fighting stopped with each side in the same position they had been in since early afternoon. Realizing an escape route was open, at 1:00 a.m., Col. Siber began an evacuation. The Confederates simply allowed the retreat, and did not pursue until the next morning. By then, Siber got away over Cotton Hill, losing only some wagons and a few of his wounded. The Battle of Fayetteville was over. A small force of 1,500 had held off 5,000 and gotten away. Confederate losses, 17 killed, 32 wounded. Union losses, 13 killed, 80 wounded. Loring did advance into the Kanawha Valley, holding it for a month before he again retreated. Taking the New River Valley and holding it were different problems.

In May of 1863, to deflect attention from another Confederate raid, Col. John McCausland was ordered to demonstrate against the Federals who had occupied Fayetteville once again. As he approached with the 36th Va. Infantry and Bryan's Battery, McCausland found the Federals were too strong for him to seize the town. The Federals had built Fort Toland on the hill west of town, protecting the road to Gauley Bridge. McCausland deployed his artillery, but soon found he was outgunned from Fort Scammon and fell behind some woods to the right of the Turnpike. Sergeant Milton Humphreys, a budding mathematician, was not to be thwarted. He calculated the range over the woods and began to fire. Humphrey's artillery fire is credited as being the first in the Civil War to use "indirect fire," firing at an unseen target, which is commonplace with modern artillery. The fire was ineffective and by 2:00 p.m. on May 20, 1863, the Confederates withdrew from Fayetteville. Later there would be some small raids, partisan warfare, but the fighting for Fayetteville was over.

Your Day One Tour has shown the difficulties that both sides had in trying to conduct a combined arms attack to accomplish their objectives over the impossibly long wagon supply lines. The Day Two Tour will show the attempts of both sides to develop a new way of war—Raids.

Stop #9 is the end of the tour. To return to Tamarack, continue west on Court Street for 0.2 of a mile to the junction with Route 19. Turn left on Route 19. End the tour at Tamarack, in Beckley 19 miles to the south (TM-155).

The Struggle for the New River Valley

The New River Valley was a minor but significant theater in the Civil War. The New River Valley posed strategic and tactical problems for both the Union and Confederate forces which played a vital role in the logistical warfare that eventually determined the military outcome of the Civil War. Nearly every military event in the New River Valley has been written about by local historians. Yet as a theater of operations, the New River Valley has been almost totally overlooked. Not a single work has been done on the whole area.

At the outset of the War, no political boundary separated the parts of Virginia. The military and political leaders of the War saw the New River as a single entity. In both 1861 and 1862, Confederates would launch offensive operations to secure the New River and Kanawha River Valleys that contained vital strategic materials, salt, and communication links. As these objectives were blunted, the Confederates went over to the defensive trying to protect strategic assets at the southern end of the Valley. Confederates would continue to raid north into the Valley for the rest of the War.

The Union forces, after stemming the Confederate offensives, began their own offensive operations that lasted more than three years before successfully attaining their objectives at the southern end of the Valley: 1) the railroad bridge over the New River at Dublin Depot (modern Radford), 2) the lead works near Wytheville, and 3) the salt works at Saltville. To succeed, the Union leaders had to learn a new way of warfare–the long distance raid. The Union success in the New River Valley played a vital role in the defeat of the Confederacy.

In **1861**, the struggle between the forces established Union control over the Kanawha Valley and the lower (northwestern) end of the New River Valley at Gauley Bridge. The Confederates dominated the rest of the theater–a line that ran from Flat Top Mountain to Sewell Mountain to Droop Mountain.

In **1862**, both sides attempted to break that line by using traditional combined arms attacks (infantry, artillery, and cavalry). These attempts failed, largely due to logistic and terrain problems.

In **1863**, both sides tried **raids**, trying to find the right formula for this theater.

In **1864 & 1865**, the Federal commanders mastered the raid strategy and accomplished their objectives.

During the four years of war in the New River Valley, there emerged a distinctive pattern of concentration and dispersion of forces linked to the seasons and needs of the major theaters of the War. In the New River Valley, key operations took place in the spring and fall. In the summer both sides usually made substantial troop withdrawals to reinforce the major campaigns in both East and West. During the summer months, the theater was torn apart by skirmishes between partisans, guerrilla irregulars, and small bands of irregular units left behind to hold the lines. In winter, the theater was largely used as forage by troops from both sides in preparation for the spring offensives.

36 THE CIVIL WAR IN THE NEW RIVER VALLEY

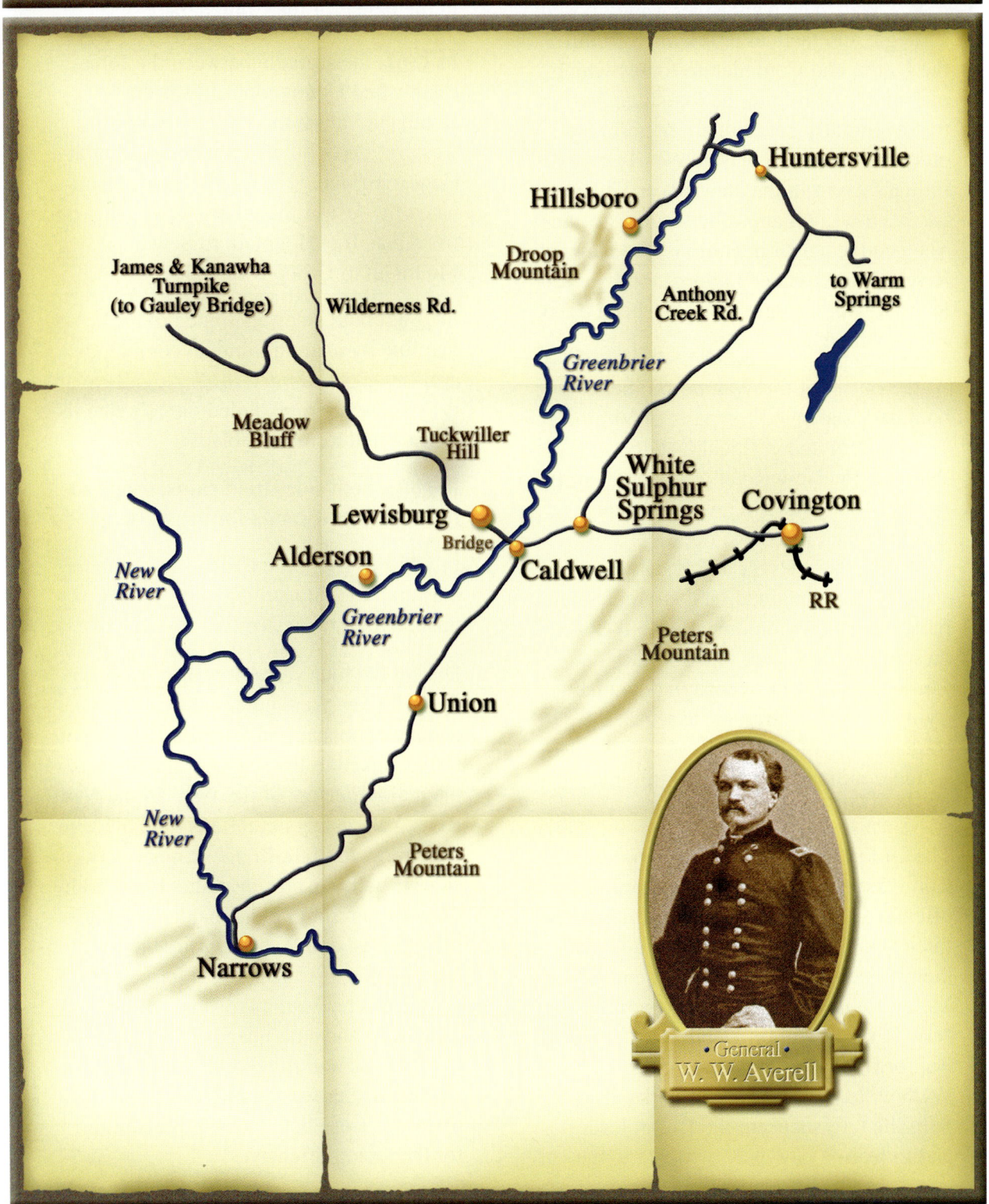

Map 12

Day Two
Historical Map (1861)

THE CIVIL WAR IN THE NEW RIVER VALLEY 37

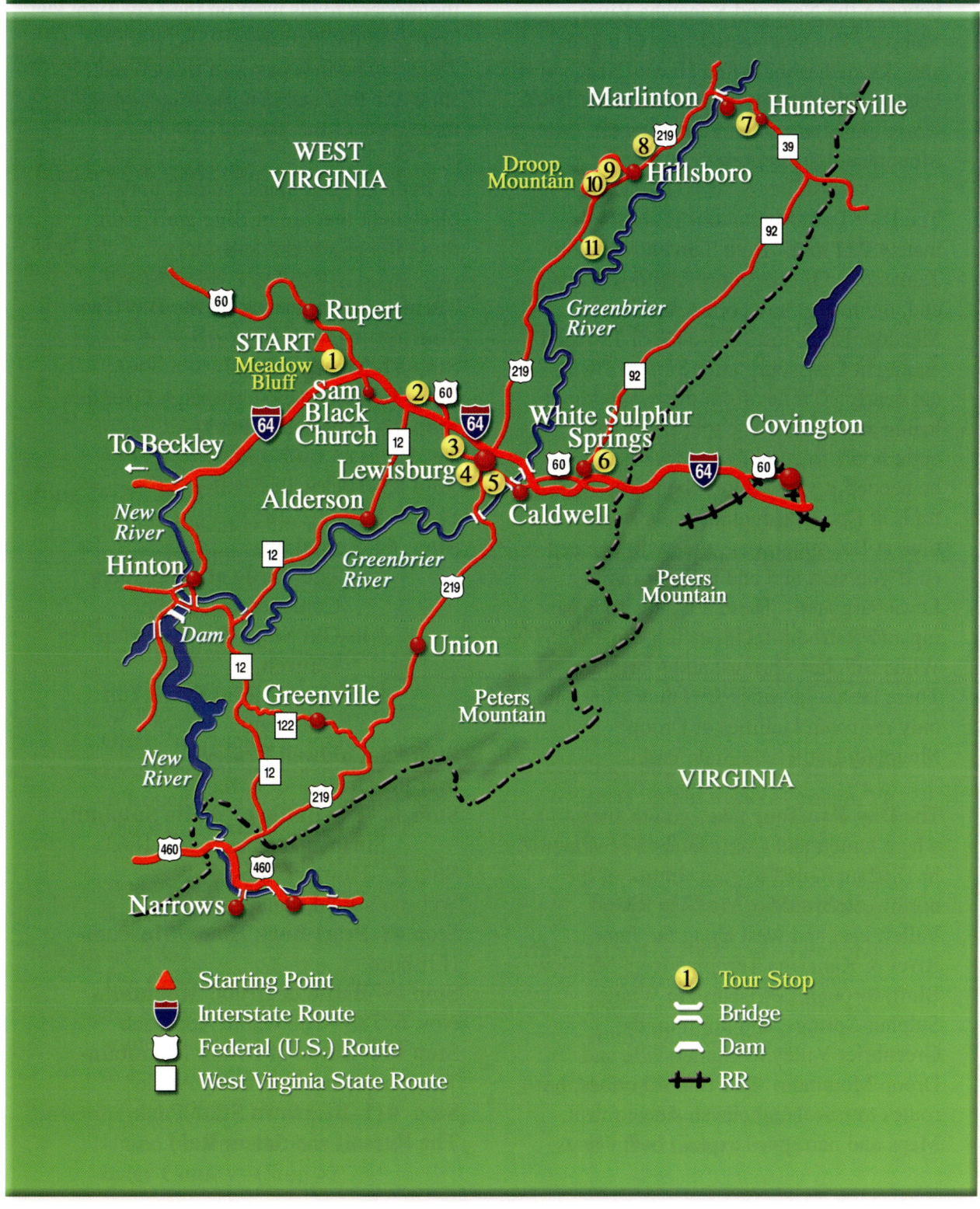

planned the approach to Sewell Mountain. October rains brought an end to the 1861 fighting along the Turnpike. Union forces fell back to Gauley Bridge; Confederates, back to Lewisburg.

In December of 1861, 150 Union troops under Major E. B. Andrews moved on Meadow Bluff by way of the Wilderness Road to capture a Confederate outpost thought to be there. Instead they found the place deserted. They destroyed 110 log huts, captured a couple of Confederate sympathizers, and carried off several hundred cattle and sheep back to their winter quarters.

In the spring of 1862, the Union forces under General Jacob Cox took the initiative and launched a strike force along the Fayette-Raleigh Turnpike on the other side of the New River, hoping to advance through Princeton to destroy the railroad bridge at Central Depot. (See Day Three Tour.) To deflect attention from the main attack, Colonel George Crook was to lead a brigade (1,400 men) east along the James River & Kanawha Turnpike, pass through Meadow Bluff and take Lewisburg. Cox was unsuccessful, but Crook won a battle at Lewisburg.

The summer and fall of 1862 saw both sides remove forces from the New River theater to support major efforts in both eastern and western theaters. By late fall, many of those forces had been returned to the New River. The raids were about to begin. Meadow Bluff would be used as a staging area for the raids in 1862, 1863, and 1864.

Leaving Meadow Bluff, return to Route 60 by reversing your route. Go 50 yards, turn right. Go 1.1 miles back to the stop sign on Route 25. Go straight ahead on Route 25 for 1.2 miles to the junction with Route 60. You are back to the Midland Trail. Turn right (east) on Route 60. Go 7 miles to Stop #2 at Tuckwiller Park.

Route 60 is the "Midland Trail" and has markers at each mile (small, rectangular, brown signs).

As you travel Route 60, there will be a number of roadside "Historical Markers." Most of them refer to events of the Colonial and Revolutionary times and Indian struggles. At (TM-52), you might want to pull over and read the sign at Sam Black Church. At (TM-54) just past "Midland Trail" marker Mile 94, make sureyou <u>stay on Route 60 East–a left turn – sign points to Lewisburg</u>. Do not go straight on Route 12.

Just past "Midland Trail" marker mile 95, pull over to the right into the public park – "Tuckwiller Park." The sign is a natural wood sign with dark lettering – hard to see. You are on Brushy Mountain. There are several Historical Markers in the area. You may want to sit at one of the picnic benches to read about the "Raids."

THE CIVIL WAR IN THE NEW RIVER VALLEY

Map 14

Area of Raids

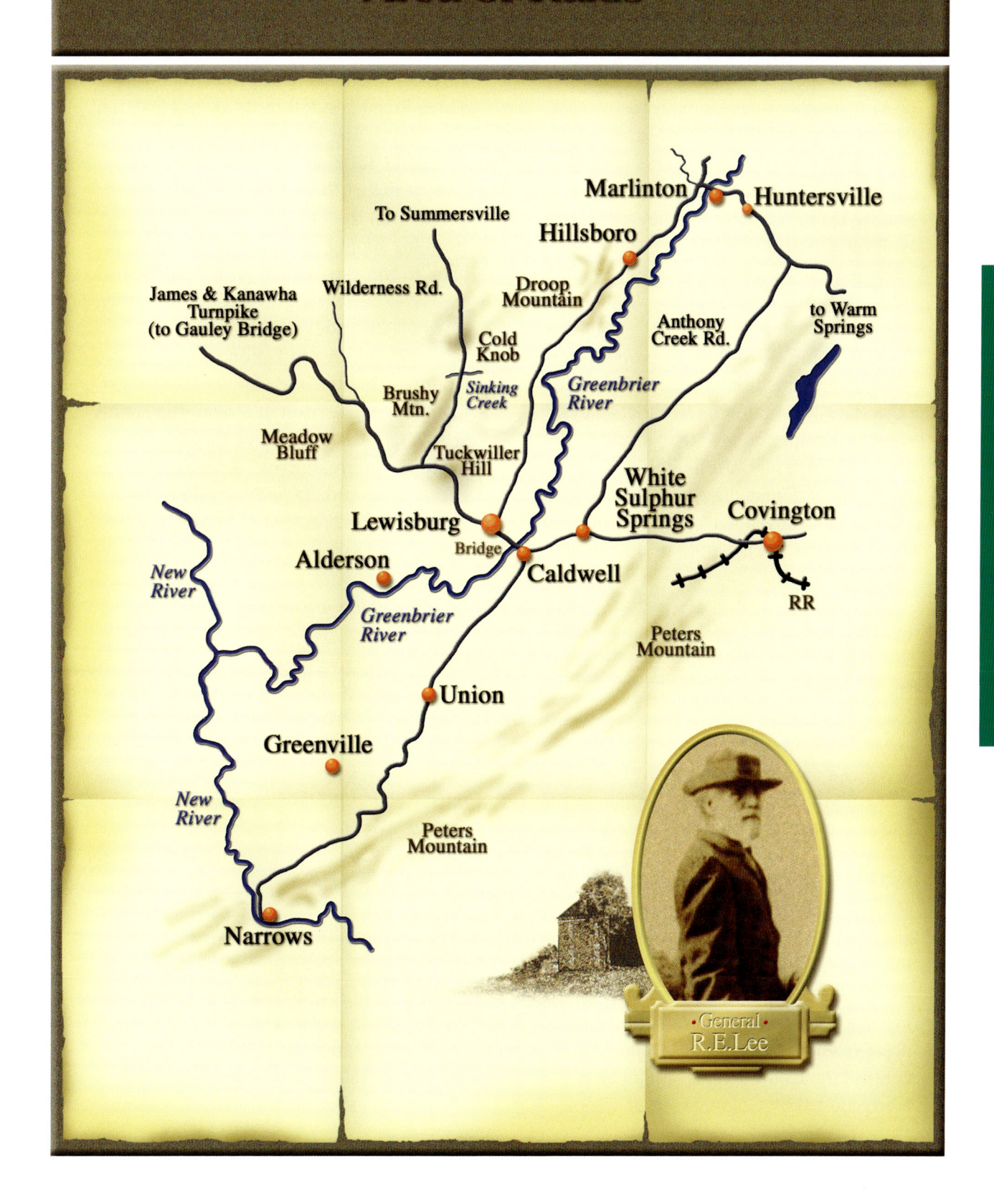

- Marlinton
- Huntersville
- To Summersville
- Hillsboro
- James & Kanawha Turnpike (to Gauley Bridge)
- Wilderness Rd.
- Droop Mountain
- Anthony Creek Rd.
- to Warm Springs
- Cold Knob
- Brushy Mtn.
- Sinking Creek
- *Greenbrier River*
- Meadow Bluff
- Tuckwiller Hill
- White Sulphur Springs
- Covington
- Lewisburg
- Bridge
- Alderson
- Caldwell
- *New River*
- *Greenbrier River*
- Peters Mountain
- RR
- Union
- Greenville
- *New River*
- Peters Mountain
- Narrows

· General ·
R.E. Lee

Stop #2 – Tuckwiller Park – The Raids of 1862-1863

In 1861, the fighting on both sides of the New River had demonstrated the difficulty of supplying conventional army operations over more than 100 miles of mountain dirt roads. In 1862, both Union and Confederates would begin to experiment with raids. None of the leaders had any significant experience in conducting a raiding tactic or strategy. They had clearly defined objectives–bridges, saltworks, leadworks, and rail lines that they wanted to control or destroy.

The problem was to find the proper force size and composition to accomplish their objectives. If the force were too small or weak, it would not have the "hitting" power to seize an objective. If a force were too large and slow, it could not be supplied and sustained. 1862 was a time for both sides to engage in trial and error experimentation.

In January of 1862, Major George Webster took a force of 738 men in a spectacularly successful raid on the Confederate base at Huntersville. We will see this raid in detail at Stop #7. Webster's success alerted both sides to the vulnerability of undefended supply bases and to the benefits of a fast moving raid.

In May of 1862, Union General Jacob Cox attempted an old fashioned combined arms attack, with his main force using the Fayette-Raleigh Turnpike on the southwest side of the New River through Princeton to strike at the railroad bridge near Newbern, Va.–Central Depot. To confuse the Confederates, a feint attack of a brigade led by Colonel George Crook was sent on the northeast side toward Lewisburg on the James River & Kanawha Turnpike. Col. Crook passed over Brushy Mountain (where you now are) and occupied Lewisburg.

Cox ran into trouble at Princeton (see Day Three Tour) and fell back toward Raleigh (Beckley). The Confederates then attacked Crook at Lewisburg. (We will look at that at Stop #4.) Even though Crook won the fight, he was too far out from his supply, and by summer he fell back to Meadow Bluff.

June 24-26, 1862, Crook attempted an infantry raid toward Union in Monroe County. He hoped to capture the Confederate garrison at Union, the county seat. Gen. Heth, aware of this danger, decided to retreat across Peters Mountain. Crook observed, *"I had hoped to strike them a severe blow by marching on them by a forced march, but they got away. We had to come back as we went, without accomplishing anything."*

Infantry raids were slow. Crook observed, *"The enemy then took station just across Greenbrier River, on the road leading from Meadow Bluff to Union, where their headquarters were. We had frequent skirmishes, but none worthy of any consequence. We had a little fight about who should occupy a blackberry patch. We got the blackberries."*

In the summer of 1862, both sides withdrew forces to fight in major theaters east and west. In August and September, the Confederates were the first to return to the New River, sending General Loring with 5,000 men (a regular combined arms force) to win back the Kanawha Valley.

Loring started by sending Col. Alfred Jenkins with 500 men on a raid, going north into central western Virginia, then swinging west to the Ohio River and south into the Kanawha Valley to block the reduced Union forces.

Loring's strategy and tactics succeeded in taking Fayetteville and the Kanawha Valley. (See Day One Tour.) The Union responded by returning large forces to the New River. By November, Loring pulled back and was relieved from command. The Confederates retreated, having learned the difficulties of long distance supply.

In November 1862, Union leaders were planning new raids. Effective planning depended on accurate information about enemy positions. General George Crook, after the Battle of Lewisburg, had set up a system of scouts to gather information. One of his scouts was Captain William H. Powell of the 2nd (West) Va. Cavalry. Using the ruse of a white flag, Powell was sent into Confederate lines to locate men wounded after the Battle of Lewisburg. His real mission was to locate Confederate troop strength and locations.

The Confederates were wary of Powell, threatened him with rough treatment, and sent him back through the lines. We will see much more of Powell as he becomes a leader of the raids and a controversial figure in the New River theater.

By November 1862, the Confederates had pulled back into Greenbrier County toward Lewisburg. On November 12, Union cavalry invaded the Greenbrier area, burning some 600 bushels of wheat and learning that Confederates had begun creating winter camps in the Lewisburg area. With this information, Crook now launched a daring raid.

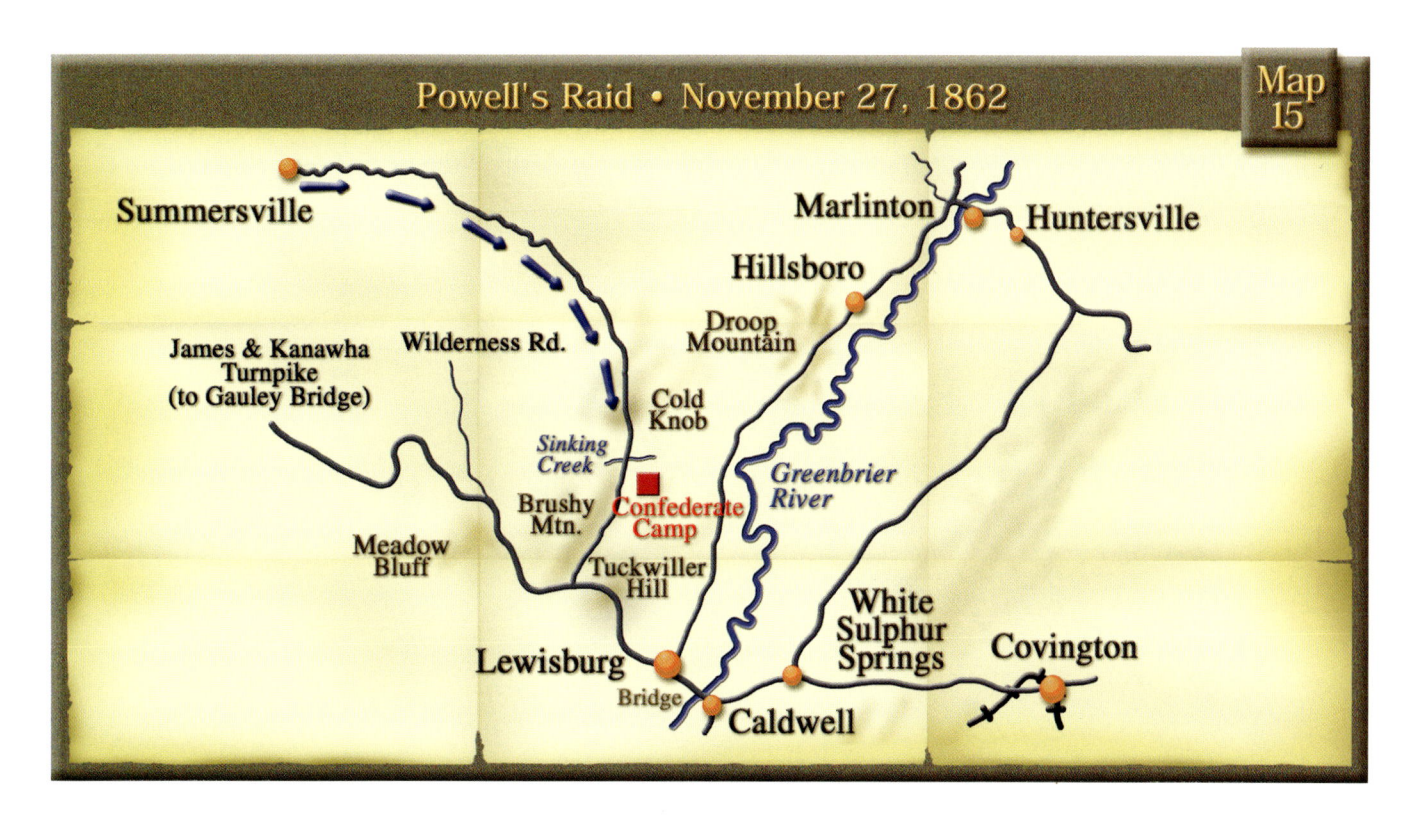

Powell's Raid • November 27, 1862 — Map 15

Sinking Creek Raid

On November 24, 1862, Col. Philander Lane, with 500 men of the 11th Ohio Infantry, and Col. John Paxton, with troopers from the 2nd (West) Va. Cavalry, were sent from Summersville on a mission with several objectives: to attack the Confederate camps, to push on through Lewisburg to Covington, and to obtain the release of Dr. William Rucker, a Union sympathizer who had been imprisoned after the Battle of Lewisburg.

By November 26, the raiders were camped at the top of Cold Knob. During the night and on into the morning, a heavy snow blanketed the area. In the morning, the infantry beat a path down the mountain toward the Confederate camp at **Sinking Creek,** some three miles away. With clothes frozen stiff and ice on their rifles, the infantry turned back.

Newly promoted Major William Powell, with *only* 20 troopers, decided to push on into the blinding storm. The Confederate camp with nearly 500 men was completely surprised and panicked. The raiders killed two, wounded several, and captured more than 100 Confederates while the rest fled. After rounding up 111 horses and mules, the raiders destroyed more than 200 rifles. (Many years after the War, in 1893, Major Powell would be awarded the Congressional Medal of Honor for this spectacular success.)

The weather forced the raiders to turn back without moving to Lewisburg and freeing Dr. Rucker. The Confederate District Commander, General Samuel Jones, was horrified and embarrassed by the raid, and Powell became a notorious villain.

Whetted by success, Crook launched a second winter raid in January of 1863. The 2nd (West) Va. Cavalry under Colonel John Paxton and Major Powell was dispatched from Camp Piatt near Charleston in the **Peters Mountain Raid.** The objective was to destroy the bridge over the

New River at Central Depot. Crook devised a rather bold plan. The regiment used the James & Kanawha Turnpike passing through Gauley Bridge to Sewell Mountain on January 13. Col. Paxton, with 100 handpicked troopers, then turned southeast through Monroe County toward the Narrows and the bridge.

These 100 were disguised in Confederate gray with their blue overcoats tied to their saddles. If they were questioned by any pickets, the force was briefed to say they were part of Col. John Clarkson's command which was stationed at Saltville. To distract the Confederates from the real mission, Major Powell was to take the rest of the regiment on to Meadow Bluff then toward Lewisburg. Powell approached to within a mile of Lewisburg where he burned a house and barn of Thomas Feamster and Austin Handley. The fire was part of Crook's plan to create a diversion. The burned buildings were on high ground and would light up the sky, allowing Paxton to sneak toward the Narrows, undetected.

The plan worked. Powell became even more notorious for this "war crime" of destroying civilian property. Paxton's 100 crossed the Greenbrier River at Alderson, and approached Centerville (Greenville) posing as Confederates, even paying a courtesy call on the Confederate commander, with Paxton identifying himself as Col. Clarkson and saying he was on his way to Richmond.

After a leisurely meal, they headed out into a driving snowstorm. They didn't dare try the ruse at Narrows and decided to try to cross Peters Mountain. Their guide got lost in the snow. They came down on the same side as they had started. By now, the Confederates were not only onto the game, but in pursuit with a full regiment of Col. John McCausland's 36th Va. Inf.

With only 100 men, Paxton knew he couldn't fight and decided to quickly head west, over Flat Top Mountain, through Raleigh Court House, back to Camp Piatt. The raid was a complete failure, only stirring up the Confederates. On January 23, 1863, Crook and many of the troops of the "Kanawha Division" were ordered to Tennessee after the Stones River Battle, leaving the New River with only a handful of Federal forces.

The spring of 1863 opened with a new set of raids. The Confederates opened with the Jones-Imboden Raids in April. Gen. Lee had ordered two separate raids into western Virginia to destroy the B&O Railroad and undermine the West Virginia statehood movement. Gen. John Imboden, with 3,400 infantry, was to march across the northern part of the state toward Grafton, while General William Jones, with 1,300, would destroy the railroad. The forces were then to join, gather supplies and recruits, and return through Summersville to Lewisburg. The raids did some damage, especially to the emerging oil industry, but had little impact on the heavily fortified railroad.

When the Confederate retreat line became obvious, the small handful of troops in the New River Valley were sent to disrupt the retreat. The 2nd (West) Va. Cavalry was sent toward Lewisburg to capture the small garrison and block the way for the Jones-Imboden retreat. The attempt led to the Skirmish at Tuckwiller's Hill–Stop #3.

Peters Mountain Raid
January 1863

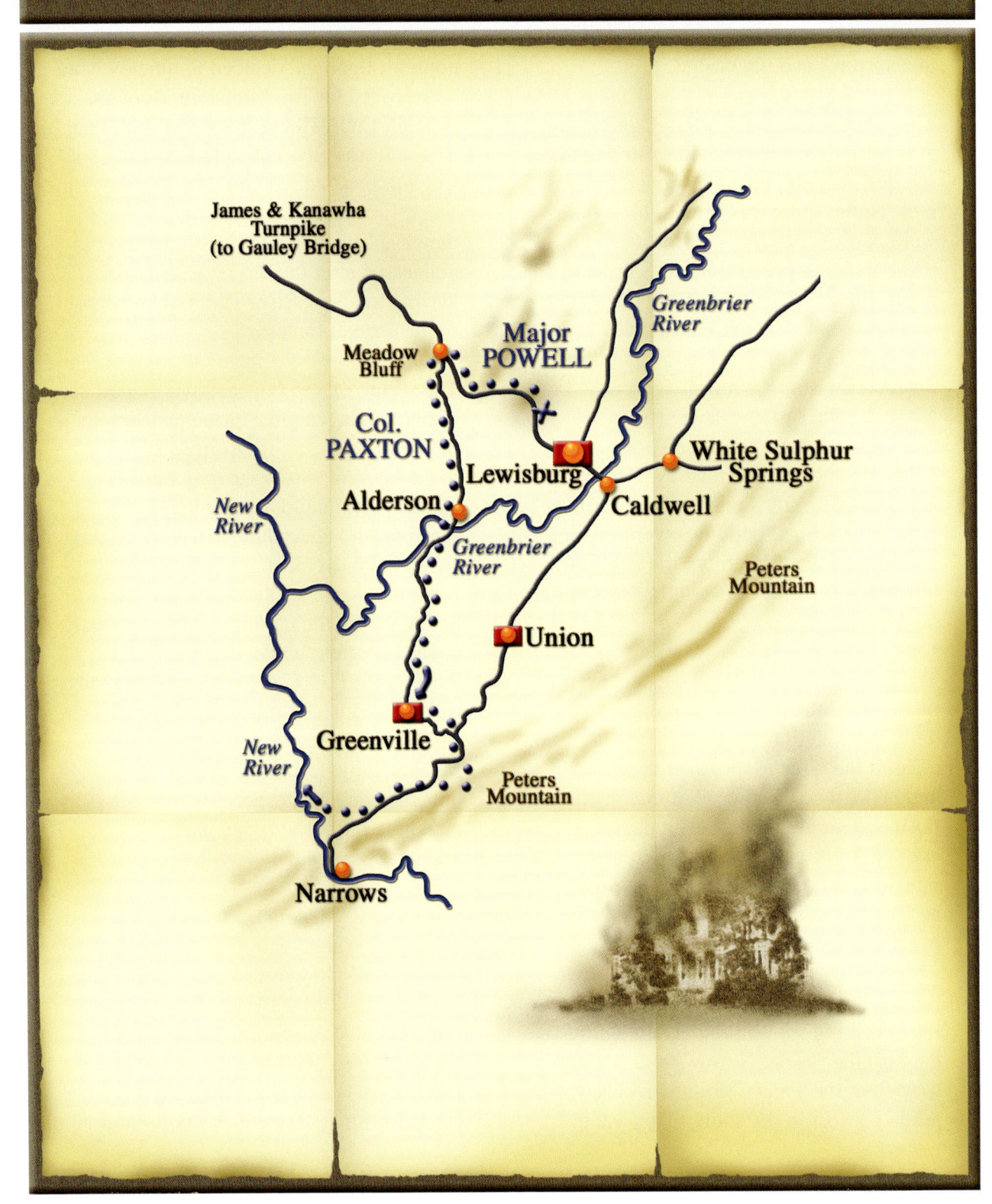

Map 16

THE CIVIL WAR IN THE NEW RIVER VALLEY

Labels on map:
- James & Kanawha Turnpike (to Gauley Bridge)
- Meadow Bluff
- Major POWELL
- Greenbrier River
- Col. PAXTON
- Lewisburg
- White Sulphur Springs
- New River
- Alderson
- Caldwell
- Greenbrier River
- Peters Mountain
- Union
- Greenville
- New River
- Peters Mountain
- Narrows

> **Leaving Tuckwiller Park, turn right back on Route 60. Continue driving east for 7.5 miles to Stop #3 –Tuckwiller's Hill.** As you start, you will be descending the east side of Brushy Mountain where the first contact was made before the Skirmish at Tuckwiller's. You will emerge into the open Greenbrier Valley.
>
> **At about 5.5 miles the road passes under I-64 and then angles to the left. Look for Midland Trail road mile marker 102. <u>SLOW DOWN.</u> Go 0.6 of a mile farther to where a yellow arrow road sign indicates a left curve. Pull over to the side of the road <u>JUST PAST THE SIGN</u>** (TM-63). **There is room to park off the road. You should see the road making a left curve down the hill, and then a right curve back up the other side. The hill on the other side is Tuckwiller Hill, where the Confederate troops were placed. (See Map 17.) At the bottom of the Hill and off a little to the right you will see a red farm house which was the Tuckwiller tavern that was here in 1863.** Now it is "Valley View Farm –The Wilsons."

**Stop #3 – Tuckwiller's Hill –
Handly Hill Skirmish
May 2, 1863**

On April 30, 1863, Col. John Paxton was ordered to take his regiment, 2nd (West) Va. Cavalry, and a company of the 1st (West) Va. Cavalry, a force of about 700 men, from Camp Piatt near Charleston to seize Lewisburg and capture the 26th Va. Battalion, blocking the escape route for Jones-Imboden. By 1:00 a.m. May 1st they had reached the foot of Big Sewell Mountain and rested until 3:00 p.m. Paxton expected he could rapidly conduct a surprise march into Lewisburg in the early morning hours of May 2. In Lewisburg, Lt. Col. George Edgar learned of the Union approach. Edgar had been wounded and captured a year before at the Battle of Lewisburg (Stop #4) but was exchanged, healed, and back in action.

Edgar's 26 Va. Battalion along with some local units only had 250 men. Instead of digging in or retreating in front of a force that outnumbered his more than 2 to 1, Edgar decided to advance and set an ambush. Edgar sent a scouting party of 28 men west on the James & Kanawha Turnpike to report on the progress of the Union force. The Confederate scouts ran into Union forces on Brushy Mountain (near Tuckwiller Park–Stop #2). The Union force informed Paxton that they had been sighted and there would not be a chance to catch the Confederates by surprise at Lewisburg.

Paxton didn't listen and continued to push forward. Meanwhile Edgar set his trap with his seven companies. He put a barricade across the road at the top of the hill and spread five companies along the top of the hill overlooking the road. He held two companies in reserve. It was near midnight when the Confederates got into position. Edgar ordered his men not to fire in the moonlight until the head of the Union column had come all the way up the hill to the barricade. The Union column would be spread out under his guns. A nice plan.

Paxton, ignoring the early warning, was marching along the road in a column of four abreast, talking, laughing, confident that they would pounce on the Confed-

Map 17 — Tuckwiller Hill • May 2, 1863

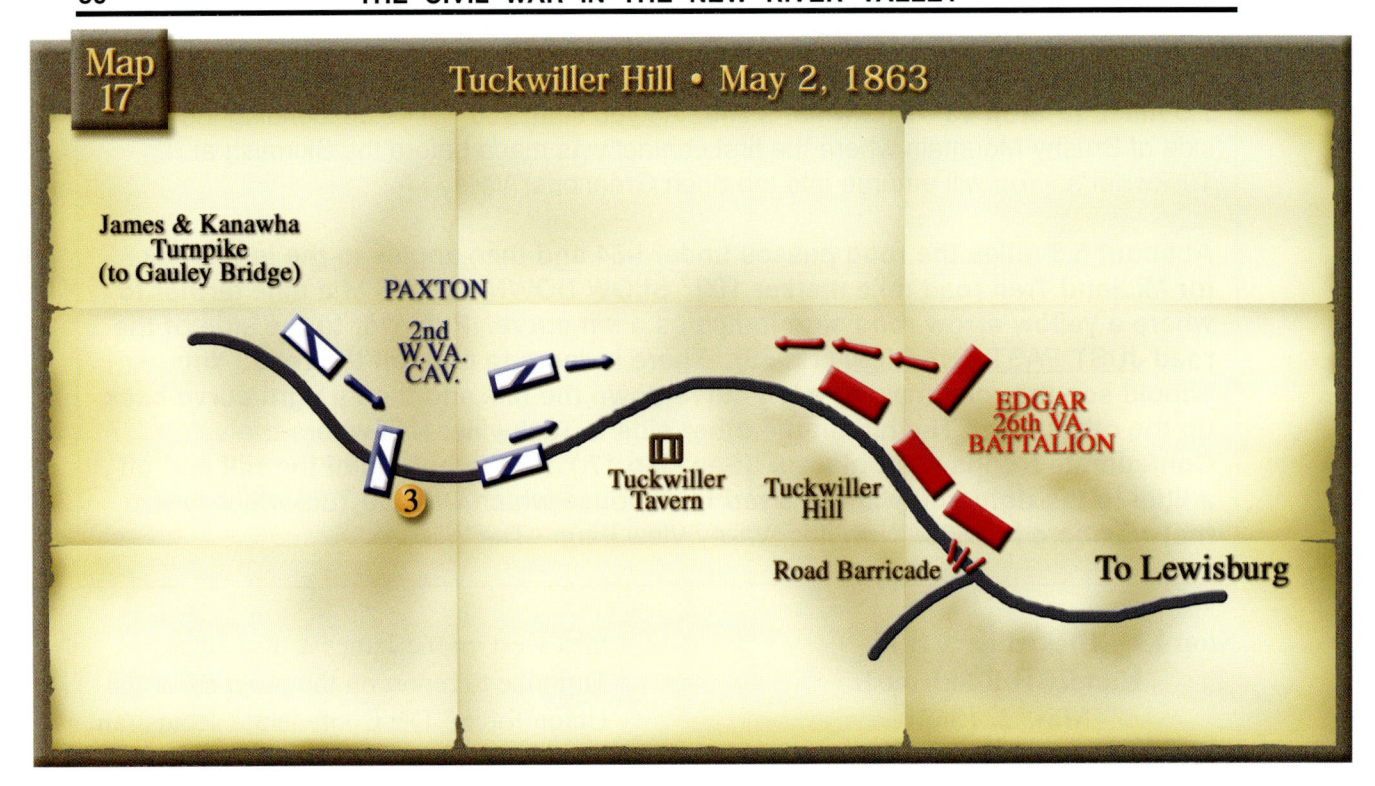

erates in Lewisburg before dawn. Just as the advance moved down the hill, a shot rang out. Someone had fired too early. The night darkness was shattered by muzzle blasts as everyone started to fire. Recovering from the surprise, Paxton sent a flanking force around to his left to get behind the Confederates on the hill. Edgar responded by sending his two reserve companies to his right, where they checked the Union advance. The firing lasted only 20 minutes. Losing his nerve, Paxton had the bugler call off the attack and fell back behind the bend in the road.

Paxton's losses were light, 4 killed, 8 wounded (2 later died), 4 captured, 28 horses killed. Edgar lost even fewer, 4 men captured. Not a single man was hit by the disorganized Union Cavalry men. In the morning, Edgar granted a truce until 11:00 a.m. for the Union to bury their dead and tend their wounded. Edgar even sent two surgeons to help. Later in his report, Edgar complained that the Yankees had taken advantage of the truce to "escape" back on the road to Camp Piatt.

Paxton did not file a report. He had been surprised by a numerically inferior force, had retreated, and in a few days he resigned from the military. His raids in January and again in May had been dramatic failures. His small, all-Cavalry force had not been able to accomplish its missions. Afterward new Union leaders had to find a solution.

> **Leaving Tuckwiller's Hill, continue east on Route 60 toward Lewisburg.** You will go back a year in time to the spring of 1862 and the **Battle of Lewisburg–Stops #4a, 4b, 4c.**
>
> **Drive 1.8 miles. Go slowly. As the road turns to a double lane, turn right–a slight angle turn–onto "McElhenny Road" 60/19, a single lane road. Go 0.6 of a mile SLOWLY. On the left side of the road there is a partially hidden little sign, "Confederate Cemetery." Make a sharp turn left on the dirt road into the cemetery. Go 0.1 of a mile; park in the loop by the cemetery. Walk around to the front of the cemetery. There are several plaques. You may enter the cemetery. The lower left side facing the gate is the best spot to look over the town of Lewisburg to view the Battle site.**
>
> In 1862, Lewisburg was a small village of about 800 population with open fields surrounding the town. Today the town has expanded, and summer foliage tends to restrict the view. The "Cross" in the cemetery is the site where the Confederates killed in the battle were reburied after the departure of the Federals.
>
> **Find a comfortable spot to read about the Battle. Look at Map 18.** There are three stops here at Lewisburg. The account of the battle is lengthy and will be done at this Stop #4a. At Stops #4b, and #4c we will look at the aftermath of battle.

Stop #4a–The Battle of Lewisburg– May 23, 1862

In the spring of 1862, Union forces under General Jacob Cox prepared to launch a combined arms attack to destroy the railroad bridge over the New River near Dublin, Va. (modern Radford, Va.). Cox planned for the main column to march along the Raleigh-Grayson Turnpike through Fayetteville and Beckley to Princeton along the southwest side of the New River.

To confuse the Confederates, Cox sent Colonel George Crook, a 34-year-old West Point career officer, with the 3rd Provisional Ohio Brigade composed of 44th Ohio Infantry, 36th Ohio Infantry, and elements of the 2nd (West) Va. Cavalry, a total of almost 1,400 men. They traveled west along the James River & Kanawha Turnpike to Lewisburg and on to Covington to destroy the Confederate supply depot at the rail head on the Jackson River. Crook's feint was to entice the Confederates to dispatch forces thus opening the way for Cox's main column. (Cox's campaign is part of the **Day Three Tour.**)

In May of 1862, Confederate forces in the upper New River were under the command of General Henry Heth, a 37-year-old West Point career officer, who had led the 45th Va. Infantry in the fall of 1861 at Carnifex Ferry. **(See Day One Tour.)** Heth, promoted to Brigade command, spread his forces from Flat Top to Brushy Mountain covering Lewisburg. When the Yankees advanced, Heth fell back to Dublin and called for help.

On May 12, Crook entered Lewisburg and continued on to the railroad at Covington, capturing some supplies at the depot. Meanwhile, the Confederates amassed a force that blocked Cox at Giles Court House and Princeton. With Cox stopped and falling back to Flat Top Mountain, Crook realized he was way out in front and vulnerable. He decided to pull back to Lewisburg. Arriving on May 21, he occupied the high ground to the west of town. **(You are now at Stop #4a–see Map 18.)**

Heth was indeed trying to cut off the Union column. At 4:00 p.m. on May 21, Heth's Brigade–composed of 45th Va. Infantry, 22nd Va. Infantry, Finney's Battalion, three Batteries, and a detachment of the 8th Va. Cavalry–a total of nearly 2,500 men, arrived at Union.

Starting at 5:00 a.m. on May 22, they marched the 20 miles to the crossing of the Greenbrier River at Caldwell, only three miles from Lewisburg. The stage was set for battle with the Confederates, having nearly twice the Federal strength in the area. Crook should have been in trouble.

Crook, being a competent officer, had posted pickets at Caldwell Bridge and had sent Company D of the 44th Ohio out to reconnoiter. (See Stop #5 – Caldwell Bridge.) At dawn, the pickets reported that Confederates were about to attack. Almost simultaneously, Confederates emerged on the hill east of town.

With only a brief stop in the middle of the night, Heth had his force on the move by 4:00 a.m., crossing the Greenbrier and closing the three miles to town to form a battle line around 5:00 a.m.

His men were tired before they had begun to fight. No time had been taken to plan a battle. That was only part of Heth's problems. There were serious command problems. Finney's Battalion had just been organized a few days earlier from militia units and remnants of several shattered units–a very questionable group.

Although the 45th Va. was a veteran unit, they had just elected a completely new set of officers not experienced in command.

Heth placed Finney on the left, deployed the 45th and 22nd on the right, and stationed the artillery in the center near the road. (See Map 18.) At 5:00 a.m., the Confederates opened with an artillery barrage. Crook could have retreated from the larger force, but did not even hesitate to engage in battle.

The 44th Ohio under Col. Samuel Gilbert was formed on the right. The 36th Ohio, Crook's original command (now under Col. Melvin Clark), was placed on the left, with the 2nd (West) Va. Cavalry in column 4 abreast on the road between his units (Washington Street). While taking artillery fire, Crook audaciously ordered his outnumbered force to attack. Crook dismounted and personally led his old unit, the 36th Ohio, in the advance.

General Heth began to make mistakes. He ordered Finney to advance across some open ground and ordered four artillery pieces to advance down the hill toward town, forcing Finney's men to lie down while the artillery fired.

On the left, near the General Lewis Inn (Stop #4c), was an old 12-pounder gun that had been taken from the British at Yorktown in the Revolutionary War. The 12-pounder did not have a carriage and was strapped between an old slave cabin and an oak tree with piled up fence posts for support. When it was fired, it broke loose, and the shot hit the brick church down the street, doing little damage to the attacking Federals.

Just before 6:00 a.m. as Finney's men moved forward, they were hit by the fire of the advancing 44th Ohio. The inexperienced militiamen broke in panic. Finney

THE CIVIL WAR IN THE NEW RIVER VALLEY

Map 18

Battle of Lewisburg
May 23, 1862

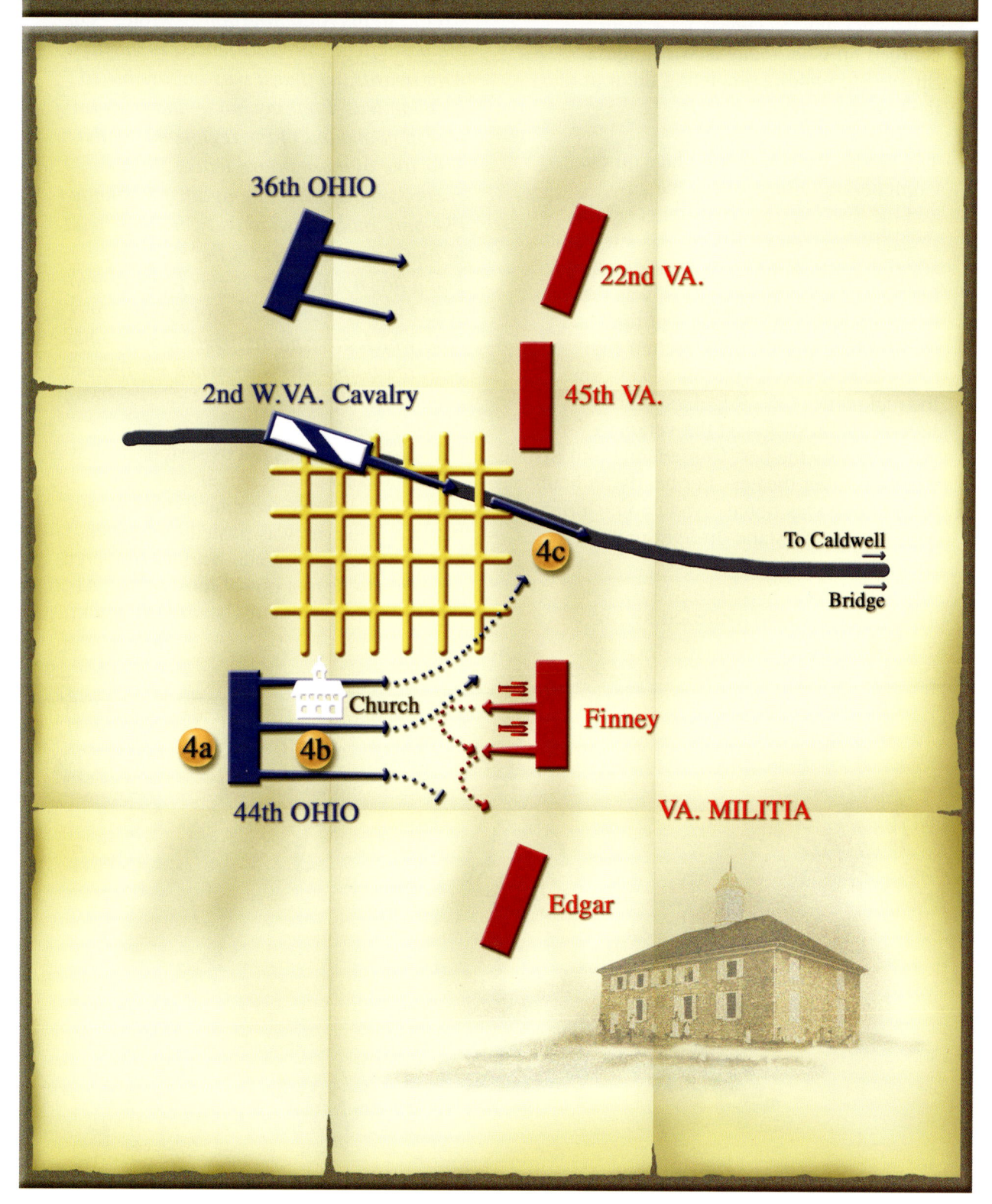

36th OHIO

22nd VA.

2nd W.VA. Cavalry

45th VA.

To Caldwell

Bridge

4c

Church

4a 4b

Finney

44th OHIO

VA. MILITIA

Edgar

was wounded and captured. Major George Edgar, second in command, tried to rally the men, but he was also shot and captured. The 44th Ohio then faced to their left and blasted the flank of the 45th Va. As the Confederate left was collapsing, the 2nd (West) Va. Cavalry charged up what today is Washington Street (Stop #4c), completing the rout of the Confederates.

The hardest fighting took place on the Confederate right between the 22nd Va. and the 36th Ohio in open fields behind several fence rows. (Today this site is the athletic fields behind the WV School of Osteopathic Medicine.) This was the first battle for the Ohioans, but they had been so carefully trained by their first commander (Crook) that they had gained the nickname, "36th Regulars." They faced a real test against the veteran 22nd Va., probably the best Confederate unit in the New River theater. For nearly an hour the fighting was fierce. An Ohio historian called it, "a fair stand-up fight in open ground."

The 22nd went into battle led by Lt. Col. Andrew Barbee, who shouted, "Come on, boys, we've got them by the umbilicus: come on!" A private in the 22nd recalled, "The balls flew like hail … you ought to have heard the balls whiz past us."

Crook, in his *Autobiography*, wrote, *"On the battlefield were lots fenced in mostly with boards, so that it was impossible to go mounted. I left my horse and went on foot in command of my regiment. Whilst near one of these board fences, the enemy's bullets striking against it sounded like hail, and, I instinctively held my head to one side so to prevent the hail from going down my neck. It was in this enclosure I was struck on the foot by a spent ball, which gave me no particular trouble until the battle was over, when my foot became very painful."*

Crook's wound was not as serious as that of Private Joseph Rollins of Company A of the 22nd Va. He recounted that as the battle opened, he was posted by a fence, and observed a comrade who had lowered his pants to have a bowel movement. At that moment the enemy began the attack.

The startled soldier began to run with his pants around his ankles. Rollins burst into laughter. While his mouth was wide open, a Federal bullet passed through one cheek and out the other. After the war, Rollins grew a beard to hide the disfiguring wound. If he had not been laughing, the bullet might have fatally shattered his jaw.

Captain John Thompson of Company A of the 22nd Va. was wounded and captured. The next day, as he was being cared for, Thompson spoke to Captain H. E. Devol of the 36th Ohio, *"I tried to kill you yesterday as you neared the fence. I had tried to shoot you three times with my revolver, when one of your men's balls came through a rail and smashed this eye out. It didn't seem to make a damned bit of difference whether your balls came through the cracks or rails, they were sure to kill or wound some of us."*

The fighting was deadly. The 22nd Va. had 395 men engaged and lost 149 or 37%. With the left flank gone, both the 45th and 22nd were forced to withdraw. Suddenly the battle was over.

The Confederates had lost 80 killed, more than 100 wounded, and 157 captured, 300 stands of arms and four artillery pieces captured. Union losses were 13 killed, 53 wounded, 7 missing.

Leaving the Confederate Cemetery, return the 0.1 mile back to McElhenny Rd. Turn left. Proceed 0.3 mile to the intersection with Church Street. Turn left on Church St. and park on the right side in the spaces facing the cemetery–Stop #4b. Across the street you will see the Carnegie Hall Visitors Center which has a good display of tourist information and brochures.

Stop #4b – Old Stone Presbyterian Church–Cemetery–Lewisburg

The church was established in 1797. The Cemetery contains more than 1,800 graves. On March 23, 1862, the 44th Ohio Inf. formed their battle line just on the other side of the Cemetery, then attacked across town and up the slope. After the battle, the Confederate dead were laid out in the Old Stone Church.

After the battle had ended, a wounded Union soldier was walking back toward his camp, when he was shot and killed by a sniper. Col. Crook was enraged and ordered an investigation, saying he would burn all the houses that shots were fired from and hang the murderers in Main Street. The inquiry determined that the shot had come from the residence of Mrs. Welch, and was fired by a relative who had escaped. Crook ordered the house burned, but no one was executed.

Crook refused to allow any ceremony for the Confederates killed in the battle, and had them buried in a mass grave along the south wall of the Church. The Union dead were buried up the hill a 1/2 mile west of town. (After the War, the 13 Union bodies were removed and buried in the National Cemetery in Staunton, Va.) The Confederates were eventually reburied in the Confederate Cemetery back at Stop #4a.

Buried out in the front-left section (D-4)

Aftermath of Battle–

Heth had made crucial mistakes.

- He had placed the untried men of Finney's Battalion on a vulnerable flank, then had them advance under fire. He should have put the 45th Va. on the flank.
- He had advanced four of his six guns down the hill into the fringe of the town where they could not be easily fired or protected. The guns should have stayed on the top of the hill.

Heth was not from southwest Virginia; thus many locals felt he had a "Tidewater Attitude." He had been given the task of enforcing an unpopular Confederate law, prohibiting the distribution of unregulated alcohol. Later in June, he would again retreat in front of a raid by Crook, causing locals to question not only his ability but also his will to fight.

Some of the locals began to circulate a rumor that on the morning of the battle, Heth had been drinking. By late summer, Heth was relieved of command in the New River theater. Later he would have a very successful career as a Commander in Lee's Army of Northern Virginia. In his writing after the War, Heth used just one sentence on Lewisburg, "A panic seized my raw troops and I met with a signal disaster."

William Finney, wounded and captured, was exchanged but did not return to his unit, finishing his military service as a purser on the Confederate blockade runner Robert E. Lee. Major Edgar, wounded and captured, was returned to his unit and led it in the ambush at Tuckwiller's Hill.

Defeats tend to bring dissension and recriminations. The men of the 22nd Va. blamed Finney's unit for the defeat and refused to march alongside of them for more than a year until they proved themselves at the Battle of White Sulphur Springs (see Stop #6).

Colonel George Crook had done well. Later he wrote, his men "could not have done better, for a more handsome victory was not gained during the war." Outnumbered nearly 2 to 1 they had routed the Confederates–so much for the myth that the Confederates only lost when outnumbered! In late summer, Crook went to the Army of the Potomac for the Antietam campaign. He was promoted to General and returned to the New River for more success.

Col. Sam Gilbert stayed with the 44th Ohio Inf. until it was reorganized as the 8th Ohio Cavalry. Lt. Col. Melvin Clark of the 36th Ohio, who had been pushed aside by the former commander (Crook) during the battle, made the final sacrifice, being killed leading an attack at South Mountain in the Antietam Campaign. The Union regiments had become battle hardened veterans.

Leaving the Inn, continue to drive east on Route 60. Go 3 miles to Stop #5 at the Caldwell bridge. Just after you pass the Midland Trail mile marker 108 — slow down. As you approach the bridge, look for a sign for the "Caldwell Boat Launch Site." Turn right into the parking lot (TM-70). There is a shelter and a picnic bench. Stop #5.

Stop #5 – The Caldwell Bridge – Over the Greenbrier River

In 1862, the bridge was a double-lane, 500-foot covered bridge, providing a strategic crossing of the Greenbrier River for the James River & Kanawha Turnpike. On the other side of the river (east), the Turnpike was joined by a road that goes south through Monroe County, to Union, the county seat, and then on to the Narrows where the New River pushes through the mountains from Virginia.

On May 22, 1862, Crook had posted a twelve-man picket force to watch the bridge for any Confederates approaching toward Lewisburg. In the night hours, Heth's column got to within a mile or so of the bridge after a 20-mile march from Union. The wagons had fallen behind, so the tired men could not have a full meal. Up and moving by 4:00 a.m., the Confederates pounced on the sleepy Union guards, capturing seven but letting a nearby Cavalry picket get away to warn Crook.

The Confederate column immediately crossed the bridge and marched to Lewisburg for the Battle. A few hours later they were back in full retreat. Lt. Col. Edwin Harman of the 45th Va. Inf. and Major Robert Bailey of the 22nd Va. Inf. gathered 40 men to form a rear guard to delay the pursuing Yankees. Harman reported, "I fired a cavalry carbine at an advancing Yankee, killing him instantly."

When the Confederates had crossed the river, the rear guard troops put bales of hay on the bridge and set it afire. The Union pursuit ended with the Yanks making a triumphant return to Lewisburg and breakfast. The Confederates fell back to the Narrows.

In November of 1863, after the Battle of Droop Mountain (Stop #9-#10), there was another hot pursuit of defeated Confederates to this bridge. Once again, the Confederates made a narrow escape and again burned a newly built bridge.

Leaving the Boat Launch Parking lot, turn right on Route 60 and continue east for 7.7 miles to Stop #6–Battle of White Sulphur Springs. Stay on Route 60 past the Greenbrier Resort, through the town of White Sulphur Springs. Just after the Midland Trail mile marker 115, you will approach the intersection with Route 92. Turn left onto Route 92 (north). There is an Historical Marker for the Dry Springs Battle. In just a few yards turn right into the parking lot of Hardee's at the Battleground Crossing Mall. Park in the first space available on the right and walk to the little enclosed monument to the battle.

You will pass the Greenbrier Resort. The resort was well known before the Civil War. During the battle it served as a Hospital for wounded of both sides.

Stop #6 –
The Battle of White Sulphur Springs– August 26-27, 1863
Averell's First Raid

The Battle has many names, depending on what account you are reading: Dry Springs, Howard Creek, Rocky Gap, and even "The Battle for the Law Books."

We jump ahead a year from the Battle of Lewisburg into the summer of 1863–the "Year of the Raids." At Stop #3, we looked at the raid that ended in the skirmish at Tuckwiller's Hill in May of 1863. The summer months once again saw forces from both sides being withdrawn to the Eastern and Western Theaters for the major battles – Chancellorsville, Gettysburg, Vicksburg, and Chickamauga. In the New River, even with reduced troop strength, the **Raids** continued with the Union trying to find the right kind of force to accomplish their strategic goals. The Confederates were also continuing their raids. In June, Col. William Jackson took a small force from Camp Northwest (at Huntersville) north to Beverly, but was unable to take the town.

In the aftermath of the Union victory at Gettysburg in early July, the commanders in the New River launched a new wave of **Raids.** In mid-July, Col. John Toland took a brigade of 800 cavalry and mounted infantry down the west side of the New River corridor to hit Wytheville in an attempt to take the lead mine. The raid was a limited success. (See **Day Three Tour.**) During the summer months, the Confederates re-occupied Lewisburg and Monroe County, even sending raiding parties as far as Sewell Mountain and Fayetteville.

In August, General Benjamin Kelley, Commander of the West Virginia District, ordered a raid from the north into the Greenbrier Valley. The new State of West Virginia had become official on June 20. Kelley not only wanted to clear Rebels out of the southern counties, but he also wanted to seize the Virginia State Law Library, located at Lewisburg. He sent a message, "The Library at Lewisburg was purchased for the western part of the State and, of course, rightfully belongs to the new State of West Virginia. Our judges need it very much."

To lead the raid, Kelley turned to General William W. Averell, a 31-year-old West Pointer who, like Crook, had experience fighting Indians in the 1850s Southwest. Averell had commanded a cavalry division in the Army of the Potomac but had some trouble at Chancellorsville. Being sent to West Virginia may have been a punishment, but it was also a chance for redemption. Thus he was highly motivated.

Averell assembled a brigade-sized force of cavalry, mounted infantry, and artillery: the 3rd and 8th West Va. Mounted Infantry, 14th Pa. Cavalry, Gibson's Independent Cavalry, and Ewing's battery, 1st, West Va. Light Artillery (six guns). He saw the need to possess and use the passes through the Allegheny Mountains that divided Virginia and West Virginia. In the next five months, he conducted **three raids,** each time learning more about the roads that wound their way through the mountains, a knowledge that allowed him to confuse and dodge his Confederate pursuers.

Averell's Route to White Sulphur Springs
August 1863

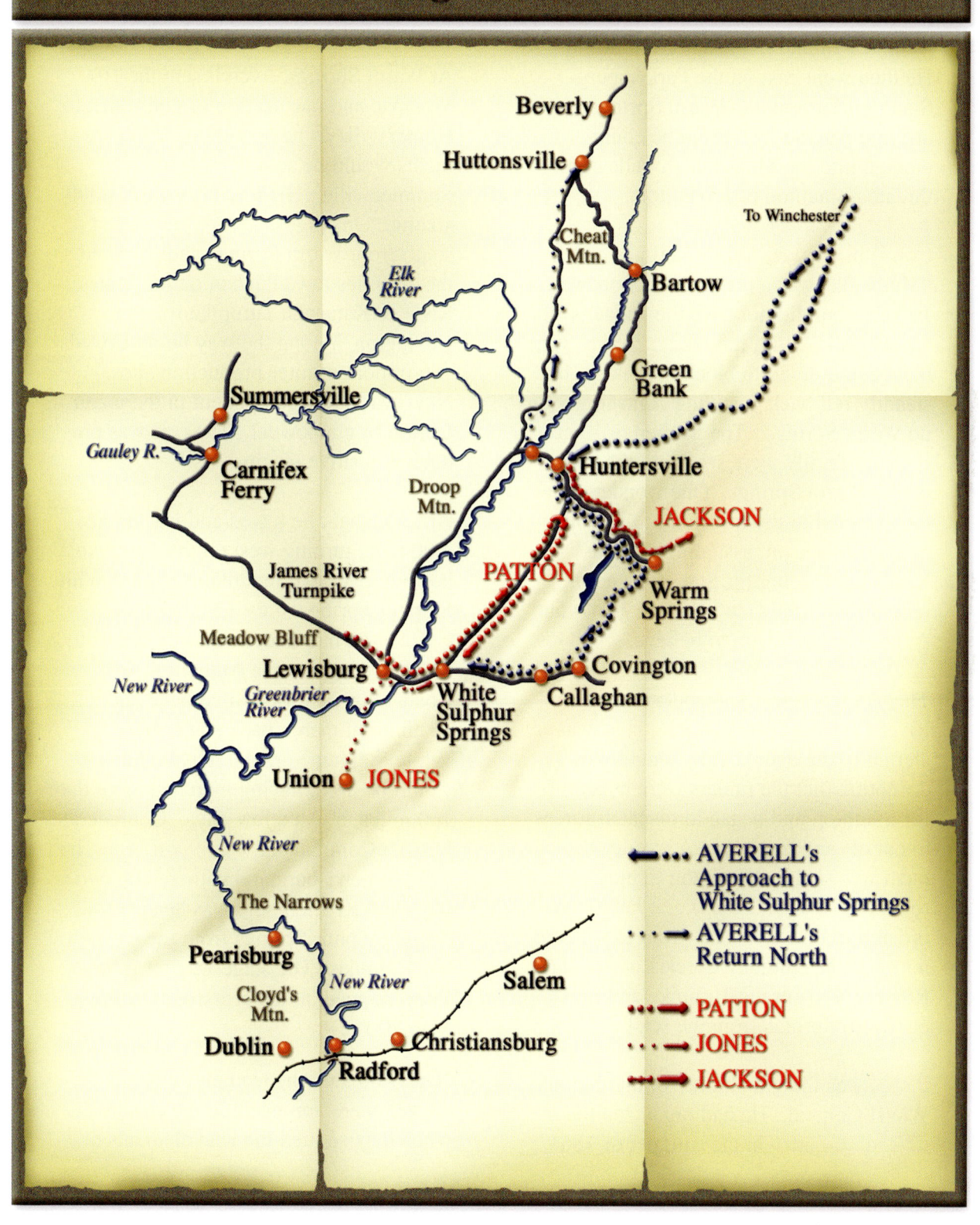

On August 5, he started from Winchester, turned into the mountains of Hardy County, moved south, and turned west to hit the Confederate camp in Huntersville (Stop #7). At Huntersville, he was joined by the 2nd West Va. and 10th West Va. Mounted Infantry, and a section of guns. He then went east on the Parkersburg-Staunton Turnpike to Warm Springs, arriving August 25. There he could emerge into the Shenandoah Valley and threaten Staunton or Lexington.

Col. William Jackson, sometimes called "Mudwall," was a relative of "Stonewall" Jackson, but did not have the audacity of "Stonewall." With the 19th Va. Cavalry, he had been ordered to block the raiders but steadily fell back, avoiding contact, giving up Warm Springs. The women of Robert E. Lee's family were spending the summer at Warm Springs. One wonders how they reacted to the invasion of Averell's column. Jackson, assuming that the Yanks were going for Staunton and the railroad, notified General Jones just what Averell wanted them to believe.

The Confederate commander of the New River District, General Sam Jones, was alerted to the danger. He bought the deception that the raiders were heading for Staunton and began to dispatch forces to cut off and trap them. A cavalry detachment was sent to Marlinton to block the route out. Colonel George S. Patton was ordered to take a brigade from Lewisburg north up the Anthony Creek Road (today Route 92) to cut the Turnpike and move on Warm Springs from the west.

Patton was the grandfather of the famous WWII General. He had organized the 22nd Va. Infantry in the summer of 1861, led them at Scary Creek, Carnifex Ferry, had been wounded at Giles Court House and missed the Battle of Lewisburg. Now, with General John Echols on sick leave, Patton had his brigade and was chasing the raiders.

At Warm Springs, Averell sent the 10th West Va. and one section of guns back to Huntersville as he hoped that reinforcements would be sent there from Summersville. His force was now **1,300 strong.** On August 25, Averell turned south from Warm Springs and marched the 25 miles to Callaghan on the James River & Kanawha Turnpike west of Covington. Along the way he destroyed two important niter production sites. Niter was a key component in the manufacture of gunpowder. The raid was producing positive results.

At Callaghan, he rested and was up at 4:00 a.m., turning west on the Turnpike, heading over two mountains toward White Sulphur Springs, only 12 miles away. Col. Patton had marched north almost to Warm Springs on the Anthony Creek Road. Now, he was called back and did an all night march back south toward White Sulphur Springs. His infantry would be tired, having marched more than 100 miles in just a few days. Confederate District Commander, Gen. Sam Jones, had gone to Lewisburg and gathered up two units and a battery and was headed for White Sulphur Springs from the west on the Turnpike. The stage was set for these forces to meet at the crossroads. (See Map 20.)

Near 9:00 a.m. the lead elements of Averell were approaching the crossroads when they spotted the lead elements of

Battle of White Sulphur Springs
August 26 - 27, 1863

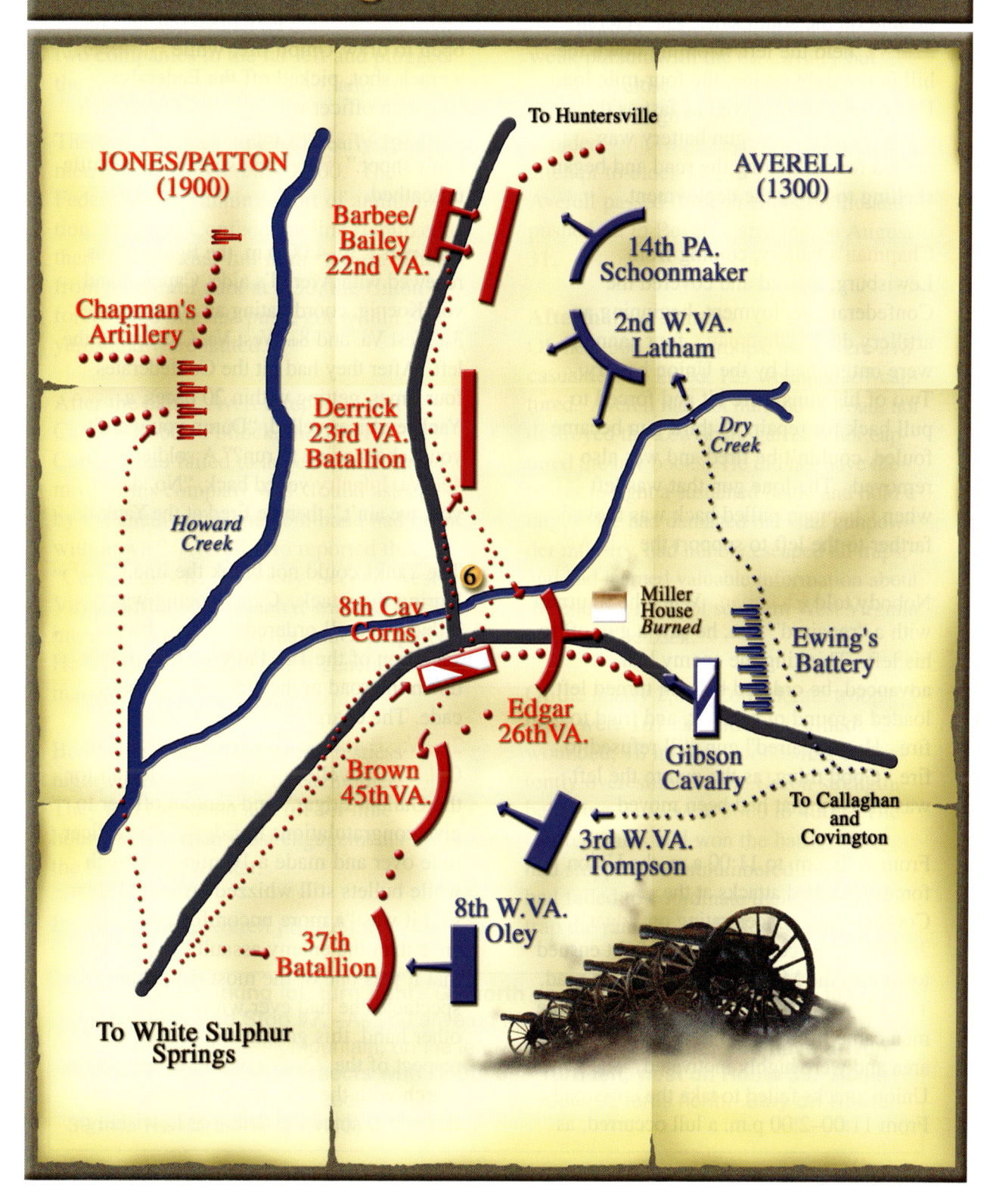

Map 20

JONES/PATTON (1900)

AVERELL (1300)

To Huntersville

Barbee/Bailey 22nd VA.

14th PA. Schoonmaker

Chapman's Artillery

2nd W.VA. Latham

Derrick 23rd VA. Batallion

Dry Creek

Howard Creek

8th Cav Corns

Miller House *Burned*

Ewing's Battery

Edgar 26th VA.

Gibson Cavalry

Brown 45th VA.

To Callaghan and Covington

3rd W.VA. Tompson

8th W.VA. Oley

37th Batallion

To White Sulphur Springs

THE CIVIL WAR IN THE NEW RIVER VALLEY

> At the Junction of 92 and 39, if you were to go right, you would be on the route to Warm Springs, the road Averell took in 1863. On the road west, after you pass Minnehaha Springs (where 92 turns north) stay on Route 39 and go through the narrow pass of Brushy Mountain along Knapp Creek. Go 3 miles to Huntersville. In the small community of Huntersville, an Historical Marker for Huntersville is on the left. Go past the marker about 100 yards. Park on the right at the lot of an old gas station/store. Across the street to your left, you should see a sign, "Beaver Creek Road," and an Historical Marker sign for the Presbyterian Church. Examine Map #7. Looking down the road in front of you, you will see the valley where the "battle" took place.

Stop #7 – Huntersville –
Webster's Raid
January 1862

Huntersville had been established in the 1820s as a trading post and then a county seat. The Confederates, early in the war, established a depot here, Camp Northwest. The Camp was on the strategic road that went from Lexington to Warm Springs, to Marlin's Bottom, up over the mountains to Beverly. Huntersville had been the staging area for Gen. Robert E. Lee's Cheat Mountain Campaign in Sept. 1861. After the 1861 battles at Gauley Bridge and Carnifex Ferry, General Loring established a forward post here. The rains at Sewell Mountain had made thousands sick. (See Day One Tour.) By December, several hundred sick and recovering Confederates were quartered at Huntersville along with a garrison of several hundred local troops.

In January 1862, Huntersville became the target for one of the first Union raids.

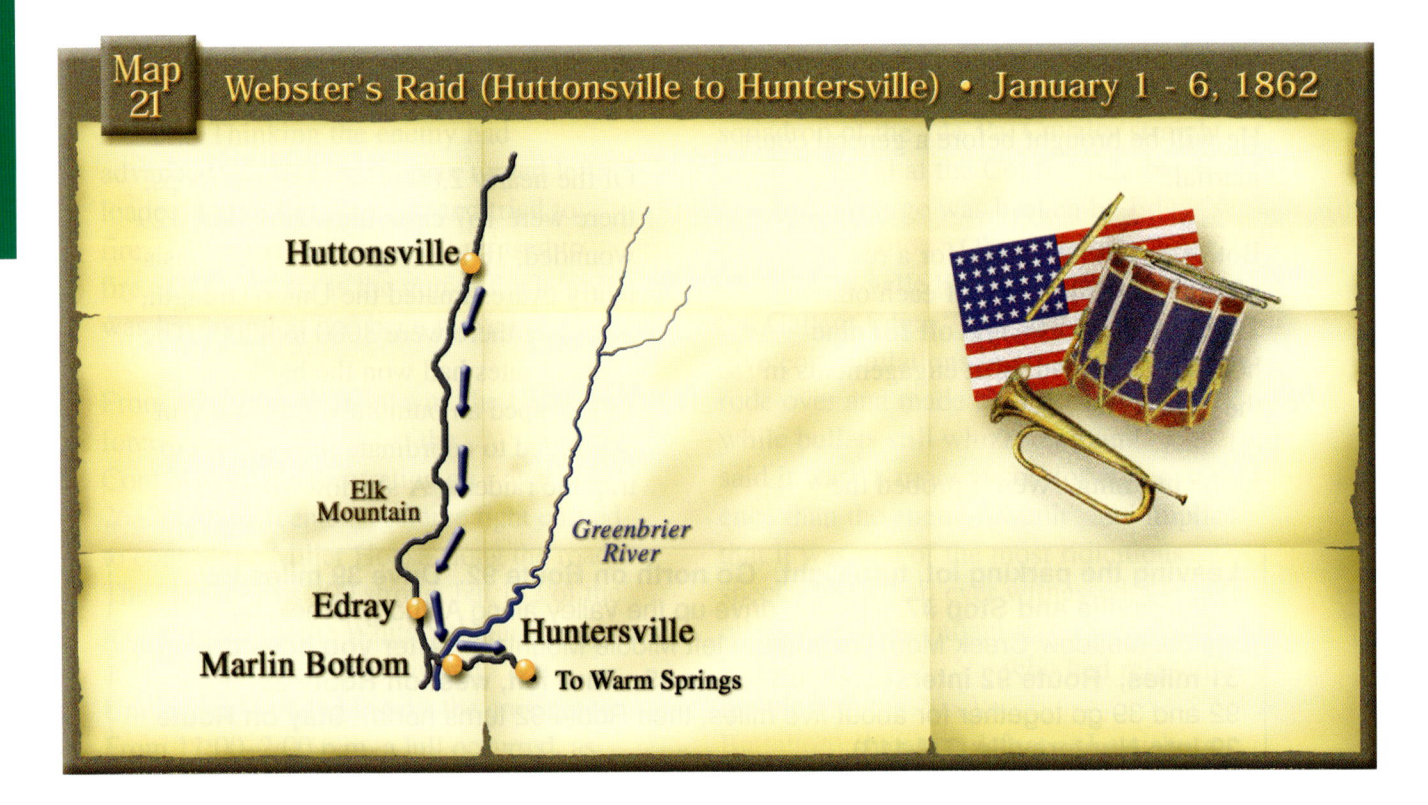

Map 21 Webster's Raid (Huttonsville to Huntersville) • January 1 - 6, 1862

THE CIVIL WAR IN THE NEW RIVER VALLEY

Major George Webster, on December 31, 1861, departed Huttonsville heading south on the Turnpike (today Seneca Trail–US 219) and by the morning of January 3, 1862, was at the foot of Elk Mountain with a force of 738 men: 25th Ohio Infantry (400), 2nd (West) Va. Infantry (300), Bracken Cavalry (38), and a number of wagons with food and ammunition. The road over Elk Mountain had been blocked with fallen trees. Webster left his wagons with a guard of 50 men and detoured around the barricades up and over the mountain.

When he got close to Marlin's Bottom (the crossing of the Greenbrier River six miles west of Huntersville), he found the bridge had been prepared for defense with rifle pits, trenches and two old cannon. No Confederate regulars manned the works. Webster saw a detachment of Confederate militia at the bridge. He sent 38 men of the Bracken Cavalry across a ford upstream to get to the rear of the bridge, while the 25th Ohio approached from the front. The Confederates ran for Huntersville. One militiaman reported "he ran that day only because he could not fly." Webster detached another 50 men to hold the bridge. His force was down to 638.

By 1:00 p.m. Webster was within two miles of Huntersville when he ran into the Confederate pickets as the road came around the bend and into open ground. (See map below.) The Confederates had been warned of advancing raiders and sent a force to block the entrance where Knapp Creek comes around Marlin Mountain about a mile from town. (This is just out of sight from Stop #7 as you look to the west along the road. You will drive by this spot on the way to Stop #8.)

When Webster sent part of the 25th Ohio

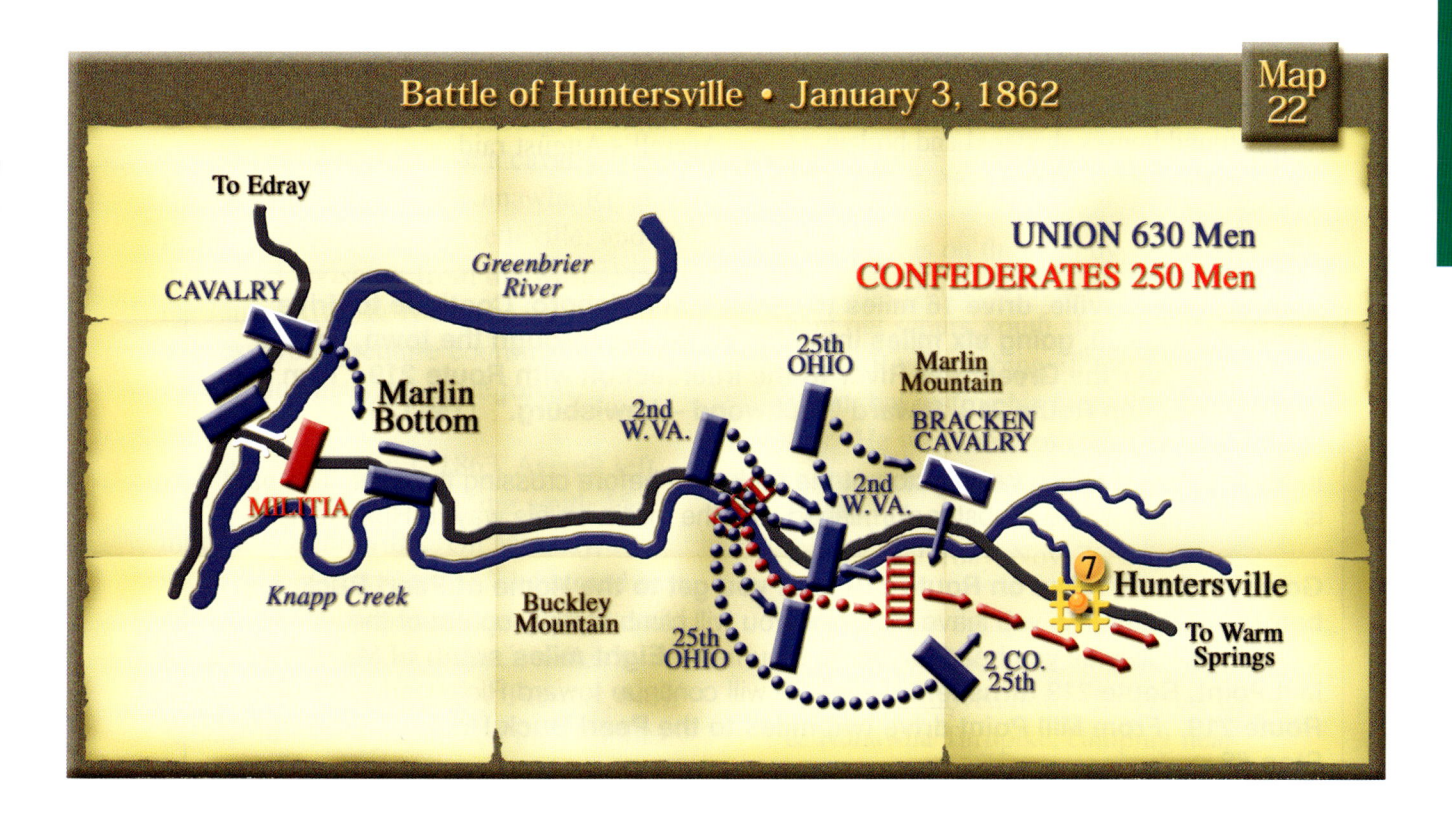

Battle of Huntersville • January 3, 1862 — Map 22

UNION 630 Men
CONFEDERATES 250 Men

Droop Mountain State Park

Map 24

From Hillsboro

Route through park

9

219

Park Entrance

10

Park H.Q.

Museum
Cannon

Monument at Bloody Angle

219

Picnic Shelter

219

To Lewisburg and stop 11 Beartown

THE CIVIL WAR IN THE NEW RIVER VALLEY

Droop Mountain Battle
November 6, 1863

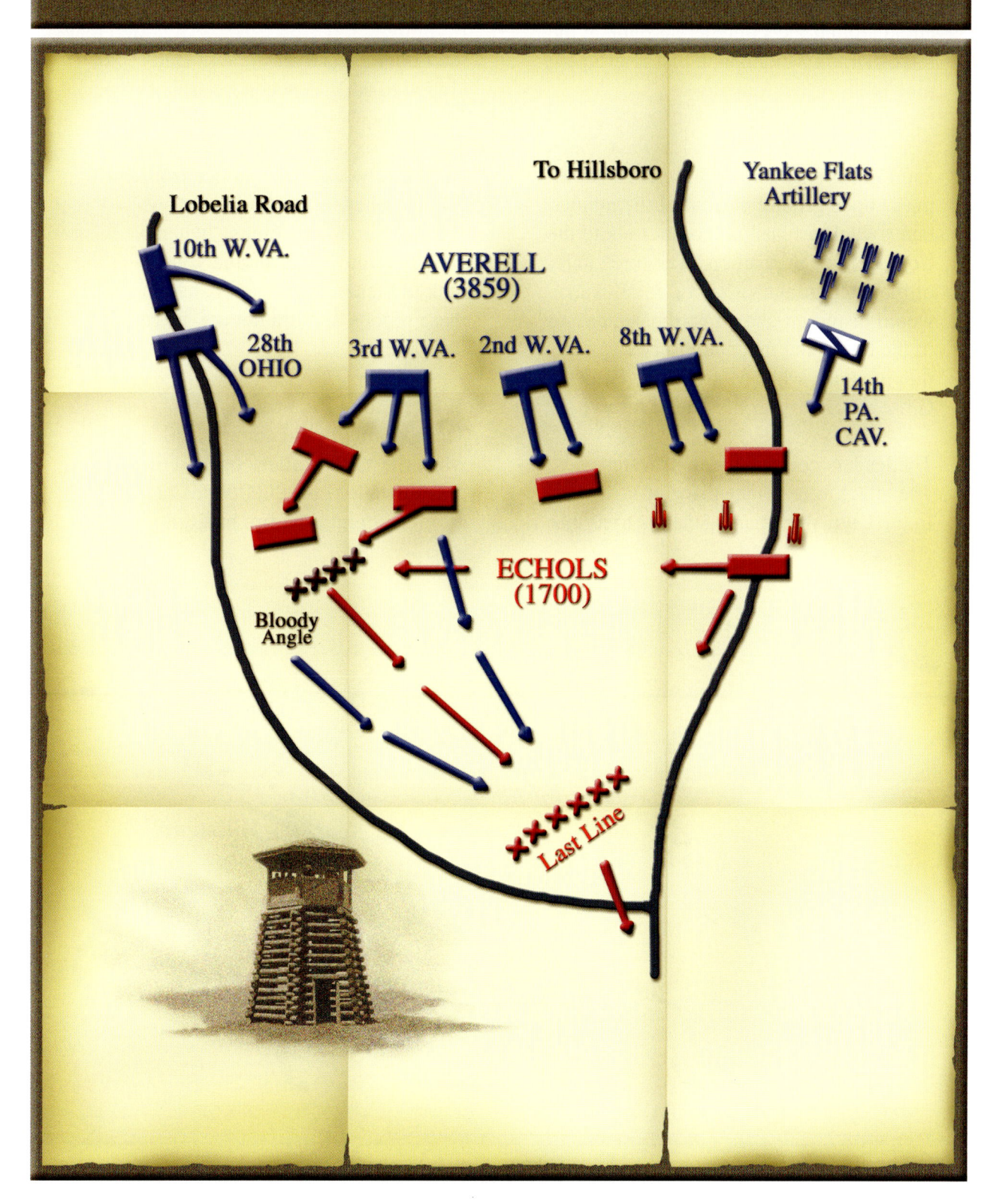

Map 25

Lobelia Road
10th W.VA.
28th OHIO

To Hillsboro

AVERELL
(3859)

3rd W.VA.   2nd W.VA.   8th W.VA.

Yankee Flats
Artillery

14th PA. CAV.

ECHOLS
(1700)

Bloody Angle

xxxxx Last Line

Instead, he planned a flank attack. Col. Augustus Moor would take his brigade of two infantry regiments, 28th Ohio, 10th W. Va., 1,175 men, back to the Lobelia Road, up the mountain on the right, and would circle around the Confederate flank at the top of Droop Mountain, a march of nearly nine miles. (See Map 26.)

Col. John Schoonmaker's 14th Pa. Cavalry and Keeper's Battery would demonstrate in the open ground in front of the mountain ("Yankee Flats"), in order to hold the Confederates in position. The three units of mounted infantry, 2nd, 3rd, 8th W. Va., would dismount and go up the center and to the left of the mountain to be in position to attack when Moor hit the flank. Gibson's cavalry would be the reserve.

The leaders coordinated their watches. The attack was to take place at 1:30 p.m. In the Civil War, many generals tried this kind of "timed attack." Usually something went wrong, but not this time. At 9:00 a.m. Moor began his march.

On the mountain, Captain Edward Bouldin, Co. B, 14th Cavalry, reported that the Lobelia Road was open. But, Echols "failed to act." A second warning came from Captain James McNeil, Co. D, 22nd Va., who reportedly was told, "if the Va. command wanted any advice from a Captain, they would let him know." Another version recounts, "when we want your advice, we'll promote you to the rank of General." If Echols had received these reports and did not act, he certainly blundered.

The shooting began about 11:00 a.m. when the Yank artillery opened the demonstration. At 2000 yards range and 500 feet up hill, the fire had little impact.

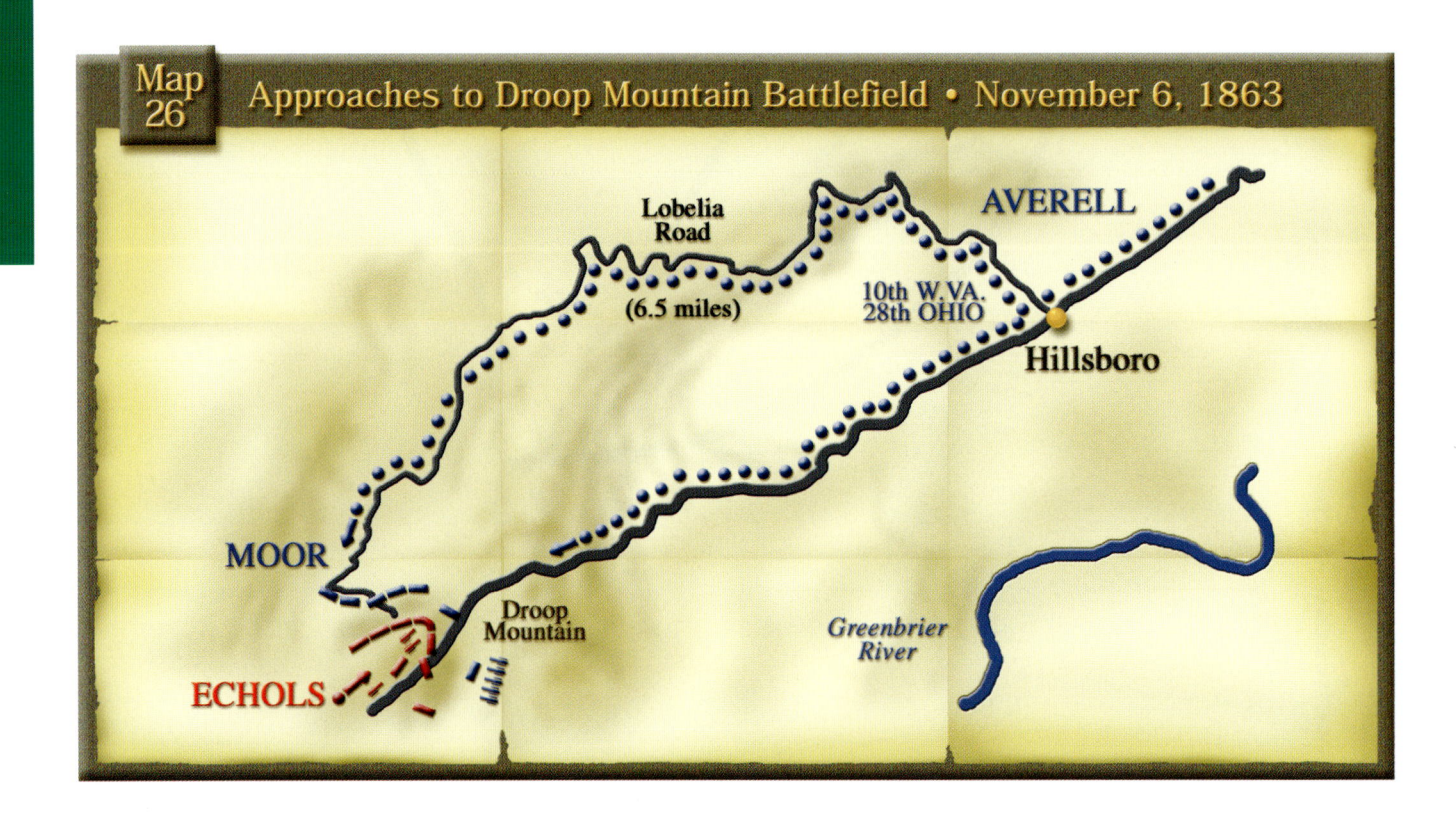

Map 26: Approaches to Droop Mountain Battlefield • November 6, 1863

View from the top of Droop Mountain

The Confederate counterfire was more effective, and the Union guns cautiously moved back. However, they got attention and covered the infantry approach.

Between 1:45 – 2:00 p.m. Moor's 28th Ohio went into battle line on the Lobelia Road and attacked the 120 cavalry men on the Confederate left flank. The 2nd W. Va. and 3rd W. Va. had worked their way to within yards of the Confederate lines in the center and left. When they heard Moor's attack, they stood and charged the Confederates on the crest. The battle was on.

Most of the fighting took place farther to the left of the modern tower. In front of the tower and to the left, elements of the 14th Pa. Cavalry did attack up the road and hill.

Leaving the parking area at the Tower, drive about a mile through the Park to Stop #10. From the parking lot, return to the main Park road and turn right toward the "Memorials and Park Offices." The roller coaster road follows the steep ravines that the Union dismounted infantry used in their approach. The "Minnie Ball Trail" is a hiking path that follows some of their route.

At the junction with the Lobelia Road, you will see the Park Headquarters. Park in the lot to the right by the Park Headquarters. Off to the left about 70 yards, you can see a cannon on the right side of the road. Walk to the cannon. Behind the cannon is a small museum with artifacts of the battle. Behind the Park Headquarters is a small cemetery. Standing in front of the cannon, look across the road. You will see two monuments. The monuments are at the site of "Bloody Angle" of the Battle.

Stop #10—
Droop Mountain –The flank attack– "The Bloody Angle"

The 28th Ohio hit the weak flank about two hundred yards west on the Lobelia Road. In ten minutes the Confederates were pushed to the rear. Echols now reacted to his weak left, shifting the 23rd Va. to the left and sending several companies of the 22nd Va. to the left. The 10th W. Va. Infantry arrived on the left of the road and attacked the 23rd Va. Battalion at the fence line in the open field, where the monuments are, "The Bloody Angle."

Sergeant Baxter and Lt. Bender of the 10th W. Va. led the charge. Baxter was killed at the fence; Bender, wounded. Colonel Thomas Harris of the 10th was leading his horse, "Old Coaly," on foot during the attack. A bullet blew through the Colonel's beard. He dropped to the ground and told his Adjutant, "John, take my horse to the rear; I'm afraid he'll get shot." The Colonel never rode his horse into battle after that.

In sending men to the left, Echols, already outnumbered, fatally weakened his center. Averell's coordinated attack now hit all along the line. By 3:00 p.m. Yanks pushed up over the top at many points. The Confederates tried to fall back to a line about 300 yards from the main road, but they were unable to hold that line.

By 4:00 p.m. Echols was ready to pull out, saying, "Yes, boys. We better go and do all we can but we're about whipped." Major "Gus" Bailey of the 22nd Va. was killed trying to hold the last line.

After the Battle, Averell wrote, *"I never experienced a happier moment in my life than when we went into the works. And the troops felt the same way. I remember one Irishman jumping up and exuberantly yelling, 'the thirty fourth fight and the first victory.'"* As the Confederates fled to the road and then south toward Lewisburg, Averell ordered Gibson's Cavalry to pursue. The race was on for Lewisburg.

Aftermath of Battle–

More than two hours of hard fighting had left both sides bloodied. Union losses were 140: 45 killed, 93 wounded, 2 captured. The chaotic retreat made it difficult to determine accurate Confederate losses. The best estimate was about 275 total.

Echols did not panic. He organized a rearguard and moved rapidly back to Lewisburg the way from which he had come. The autumn darkness fell quickly. The Yanks pursued for five miles, ran into the rearguard going down the other side of the mountain and halted for the night.

Where was Duffie with his fresh 2,500 men and five guns? By 3:00 as the battle raged, Duffie had moved from Meadow Bluff to Muddy Creek Mountain about seven miles from Lewisburg. But he was not supposed to be in Lewisburg until afternoon the next day. He halted.

We will look at the pursuit after the next Stop.

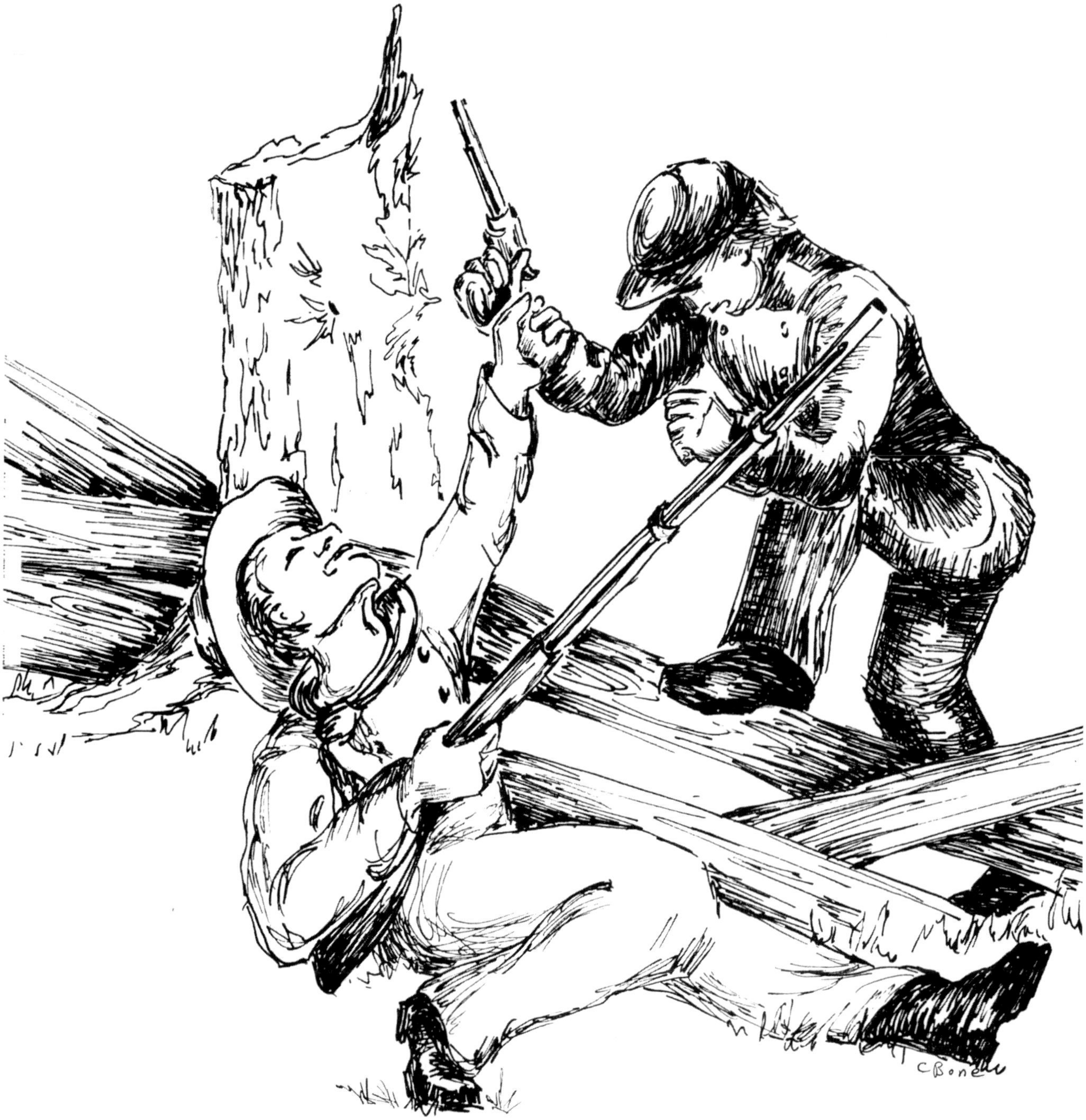

The Fratricidal Battle:
"Brother *versus* Brother"

Most of the conflicts in the New River Theater involved family and neighbors fighting on opposite sides in this extremely divided territory. More than 80 fought each other at Droop Mountain.

Three examples:

• At the end of the Battle, a Union Pvt. Alfred McKeever, 3rd W. Va., recognized a captured Rebel as his half-brother, Capt. James McNeil, 22nd Va., and went to him with outstretched arms. The Confederate responded, "I am glad to know, Alfred, that you are alive and well, but Alfred, we are not shaking hands today."

• In a more ironic twist, another Yank was sent to guard a prisoner who turned out to be his father. Another soldier expressed concern that the son might let the father run away. The son exclaimed, "Father knows better than to try and get away, as he knows I would have to do my duty in that case."

• On a more tragic note, Pvt. Andrew Short, 10th W. Va., helped gather bodies after the battle in the dark. Asking for a light, he noticed a crooked finger, then discovered that the body was that of Pvt. John Short, 22nd Va.–his brother!

Leaving Stop # 10 drive 5 miles to Beartown State Park, Stop #11. To leave the Park, continue on the Park road, going past the cannon. After 0.3 mile, bear left just before the picnic area, go to the stop sign to leave the Park. Turn right, south, on Route 219 (TM-113). Drive three miles. Go slowly. Look for the sign for Beartown, "A Natural Area." Turn left. Go 2 miles until the road ends at the parking lot at Beartown State Park. Beartown is not a Civil War site. If you do not have time, this Stop may be bypassed. However, it is an enchanting place and should not be missed when you are this close. Beartown is closed Oct. – April.

Stop #11

Beartown State Park

Beartown contains 107 acres of unusual rock formations. Visitors can take a nonstrenuous walk on a boardwalk that has interpretive signs explaining the formations. Whatever the season or weather, Beartown provides a relaxing respite back into nature. The walk will take 30-45 minutes. There is no charge. There are only basic toilet facilities at the parking area.

Leaving Beartown, return to Route 219; turn left, south; drive 22 miles to the intersection with Interstate 64. Turn right on I-64, west to return to Beckley. Tamarack is 55 miles (TM-196).

There are no "Stops" after Beartown. You may want to read the concluding materials at Beartown or during the 22-mile drive back to Lewisburg. You may end the tour at Lewisburg, or return to Beckley.

Pursuit and conclusion to Averell's Second Raid–

The Yankee pursuit slowed down by 9:00 p.m. near the Renick House (about 8.4 miles south of Beartown on Route 219). The house was the home of a Confederate killed in the nearby rearguard fighting. The limestone portion of the house was started in 1787, and the brick portion completed in 1825. John Renick was a Confederate officer. At the outset of the war, his farm was prosperous, with 300 cattle, 1,000 sheep, 200 hogs, 125 horses, and a large number of slaves.

Echols' forces pushed on in the dark, going several more miles past Renick to Frankford, where they took a couple hours of needed rest. At 3:00 a.m. on Saturday, Nov. 7, Echols, having learned that Duffie was near Lewisburg, got his tired men back on the road, passed through Lewisburg without stopping and continued to the Caldwell Bridge, arriving between 8:00 – 9:00 a.m. The Confederates had taken 24 hours to march the 28 miles to Droop Mountain, but only 11 hours to return. They had marched 56 miles in 42 hours and been in battle at Droop Mountain.

Lt. Micah Woods reported, *"Our escape must only be attributed to our rapid running. The whole distance from the battlefield to Greenbrier bridge – 32 miles – was made at a full trot and often at a full run. Hundreds of infantry and dismounted men took to the bushes and large numbers who are infantry will come up."*

If Averell or Duffie had moved as quickly, they might have trapped and destroyed the defeated Confederates. Duffie arrived at Lewisburg only minutes after the last Confederates were gone. He pushed on to the bridge over the Greenbrier only to see it go up in flames as had happened a year earlier after the Battle of Lewisburg. The Confederates had once again gotten away. Duffie returned to Lewisburg where his troops ravaged the town.

When Averell arrived, and realized the Confederates were gone, he faced some hard choices. He had won a victory, but the Confederates had escaped. His fighting power had been diminished. He ordered Duffie to pursue the Confederates south into Monroe County, sent his infantry back to Beverly by way of Droop Mountain to pick up the wounded, and then marched east toward White Sulphur Springs and Covington with his mounted forces.

The Confederates had begun to respond to the invasion threat. Generals Imboden and Jones were belatedly sending forces from the Shenandoah to trap and destroy the raiders. On a snowy Monday, Nov. 9, at Covington, Averell realized the danger and decided he could not push through to destroy the railroad. He turned north and made his way back to the Union bases by Nov. 17, escaping several attacks on his column on the way.

Once again, as after White Sulphur Springs, Averell gained more knowledge of the back roads through the mountains that divided Virginia and West Virginia. Averell's Second Raid was over, but he would be back. Duffie did not pursue into Monroe County, retreating instead to Meadow Bluff, and then back to Charleston.

THE CIVIL WAR IN THE NEW RIVER VALLEY

Conclusion–

Averell had won a battle victory. West Virginia Statehood seemed assured. He did not get even close to his target–the railroad. He should have been able to catch the routed Confederates. The two Union generals bickered over who was at fault.

The Confederates had lost a battle. Echols' army had been hurt and scattered, but not destroyed. Within ten days, the Confederates had re-occupied their former positions at Lewisburg and the eastern New River Valley. The struggle would continue.

The David Creigh Incident

There are several versions of this incident, but the basic story begins on Nov. 8, 1863, as the Confederates defeated at Droop Mountain were fleeing south. A union soldier, most likely one of Duffie's troopers, was pillaging homes just south of Lewisburg. He went into the home of David Creigh, insulted the women and was plundering the attic. Creigh confronted him. The soldier drew his gun, so did Creigh. Both fired, then scuffled, falling down the stairs. A black woman servant handed Creigh an axe. Creigh then dispatched the marauder and hid the body.

A year later, when Averell returned after the Cloyd's Mountain Battle, a young black boy reported the incident. Creigh was arrested, given a mock trial, and executed. War created pain and a legacy of hate and sorrow. Creigh was buried in the Lewisburg cemetery.

Averell's Third Raid
The Salem Raid, December 1863

In December 1863, General Longstreet was besieging General Burnside at Knoxville, Tennessee, and was using the Va. & Tenn. Railroad as a supply line. General William Averell was ordered to cut the line and disrupt the Confederate supply. Having learned from his two unsuccessful attempts in August and November, Averell carefully planned a raid which made critical use of deception. (See Map 27.) His main column, consisting of the experienced mounted infantry and cavalry with Ewing's guns, were covered by three feints.

General Scammon took his brigade from Charleston to Lewisburg. Col. Moore took his infantry from Beverly to Hillsboro and joined the threat to Lewisburg. Col. George Wells took two infantry regiments from Harpers Ferry and moved toward Staunton. Averell's fast moving column, which used lesser known back roads between mountains, was shielded by the very visible feints.

The Raid was underway on December 8. The Confederate command, completely confused, believed Staunton was the objective. Nearly 12,000 Confederate troops were put in motion to catch the raiders. When the main Union column reached Callaghan, they feinted toward Staunton. In freezing rain they turned south through the mountains to New Castle and emerged at Salem near noon on Dec. 16, completely fooling the Confederates.

THE CIVIL WAR IN THE NEW RIVER VALLEY

Averell's Third Raid • Salem Raid
December 8 - 24, 1863

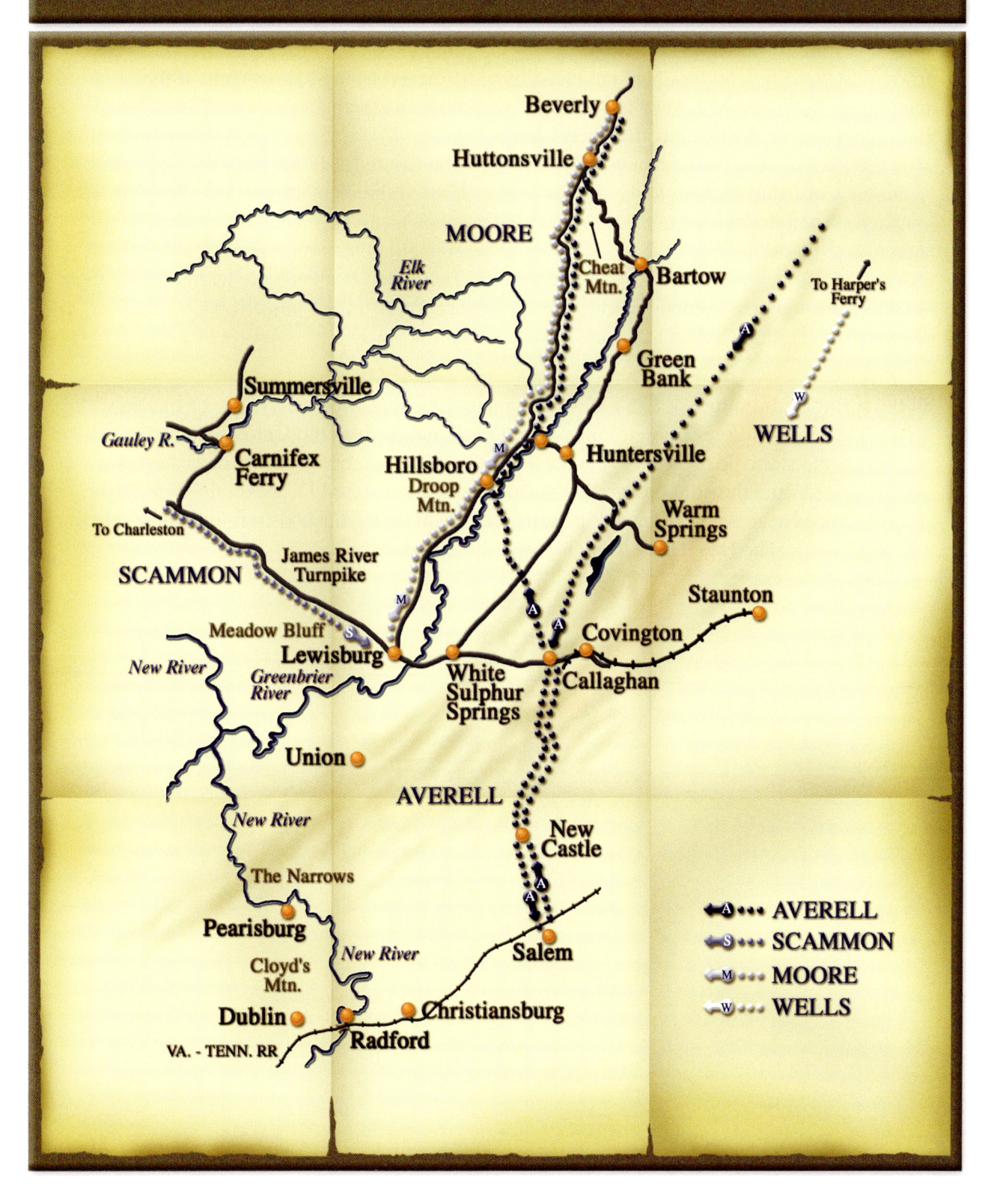

Map 27

The raiders arrived just as a troop train was approaching. Two 3-inch guns fired into the train, which backed away as fast as possible. For the next four hours Averell's men destroyed supplies stockpiled for Longstreet. They tore up more than four miles of track on either side of town, destroyed five bridges, and cut the telegraph. Before leaving town at 4:00 p.m. the raiders dropped hints that they would retreat by way of Buchanan. Once again the Confederates bought the deception and rushed the pursuit in the wrong direction.

Averell retreated on his same line of approach, changing what he had done on his first raids. Just past Callaghan, he ran into a weak force of "Mudwall" Jackson, which he pushed aside without injury. Averell then turned to Hillsboro and was back at Beverly on December 24. He had marched 400 miles and had not lost one man in combat. (Seven, however, were drowned trying to cross one of the flooded streams.)

The Confederate *Richmond Examiner* blasted the inept attempts to catch the raiders, saying, "The great Averell had gone, not up spout, but back to his den." The Union leaders were learning how to accomplish their objectives.

In the spring and summer of 1864, Lewisburg and the Greenbrier Valley side of the New River Theater would see Union troops passing back and forth as the Union renewed the attacks on the strategic objectives, but there would be little fighting as the focus shifted south. In 1864 the thrust to destroy the railroad bridge at Central Depot on the New River, the lead mines near Wytheville, and the salt works would be launched from the *other* side of the New River. The **Day Three Tour** looks at these attacks.

The Struggle for the New River Valley

The New River Valley was a minor but significant theater in the Civil War. The New River Valley posed strategic and tactical problems for both the Union and Confederate forces which played a vital role in the logistical warfare that eventually determined the military outcome of the Civil War. Nearly every military event in the New River Valley has been written about by local historians. Yet, as a theater of operations, the New River Valley has been almost totally overlooked. Not a single work has ever been done on the whole area.

At the outset of the War, no political boundary separated the parts of Virginia. The military and political leaders of the War saw the New River as a single entity. In both 1861 and 1862, Confederates launched offensive operations to secure the lower New River and Kanawha River valleys that contained vital strategic materials, salt, lead, and communications links. As these offensives were blunted, the Confederates went over to the defensive trying to protect strategic assets at the southern (upper) end of the valley. Confederates would continue to raid north into the Valley.

The Union forces, after stemming the Confederate offensives, began their own offensive operations that lasted more than three years before successfully attaining their objectives in the southern end of the Valley: the railroad bridge over the New River at Central Depot (Radford), the lead works near Wytheville, and the salt works at Saltville. To succeed, the Union forces had to learn a new way of warfare — the long distance raid. The Union success in the New River Valley played a vital role in the defeat of the Confederacy.

In **1861** the struggle between the forces established Union control over the Kanawha Valley and Gauley Bridge. Confederates dominated the rest of the theater – a line that ran from Flat Top Mountain to Sewell Mountain to Droop Mountain.

In **1862** both sides attempted traditional combined arms (infantry, artillery, and cavalry) offensives to break the line. These attempts failed, largely due to logistic and terrain problems.

In **1863** both sides turned to **raids,** trying to find the right formula for this theater. In **1864** and **1865** the Federal forces mastered the raid strategy and accomplished their objectives.

During the four years of war in the New River Valley, there was a distinctive pattern of concentration and dispersion of forces linked to the seasons and needs of the major theaters of the War. In the New River Valley, major operations took place in the spring and fall. In the summer, both sides usually made substantial troop withdrawals to reinforce the major campaigns in both East and West. During the summer months, the theater was torn apart by skirmishes between partisans, guerilla irregulars, and small regular units left behind to hold the lines. In winter, the theater was largely used as forage by troops from both sides in preparation for a spring offensive.

Day Three
Historical Map (1862-1864)

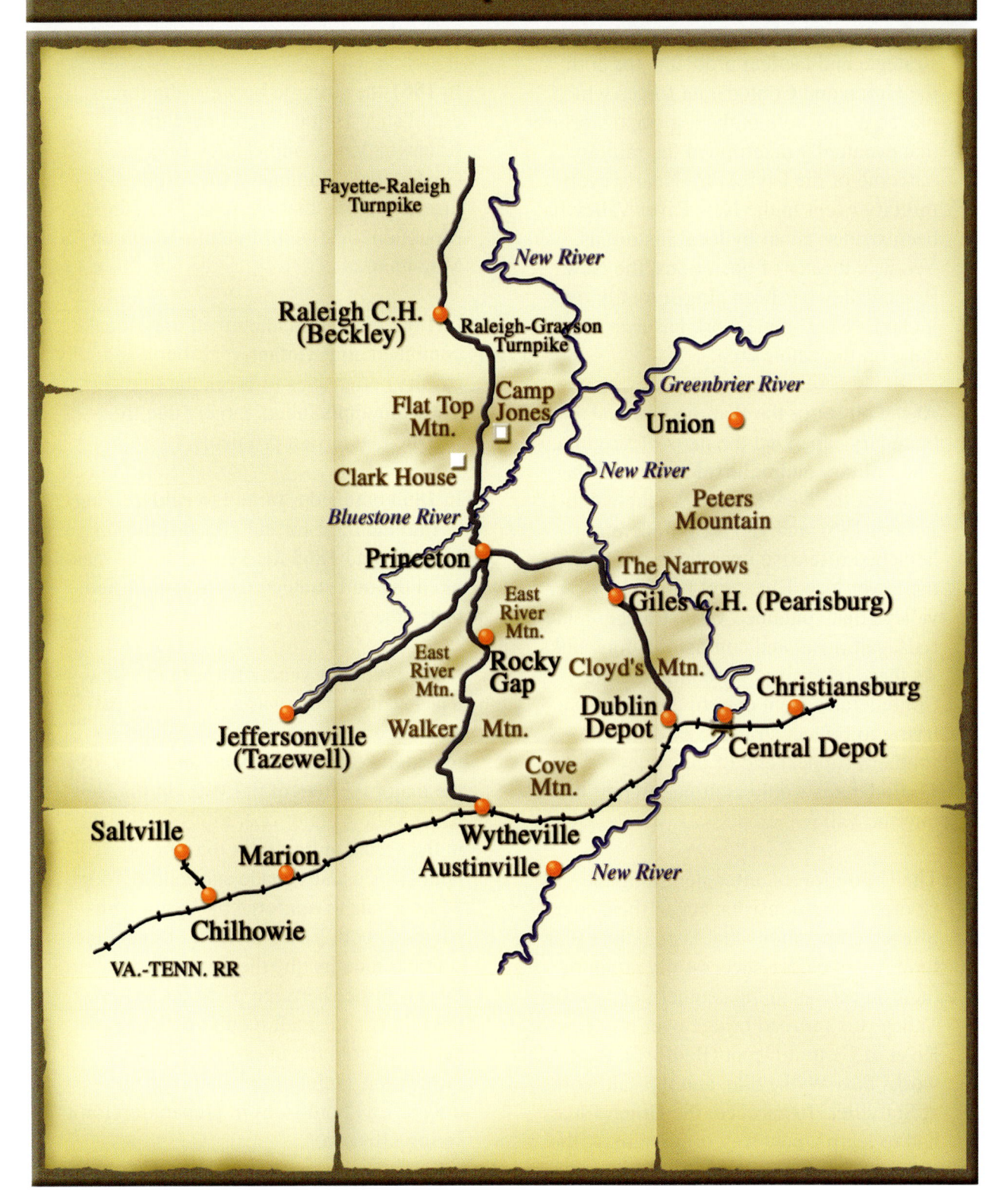

Map 28

THE CIVIL WAR IN THE NEW RIVER VALLEY 85

Day Three
Modern Roads

Map 29

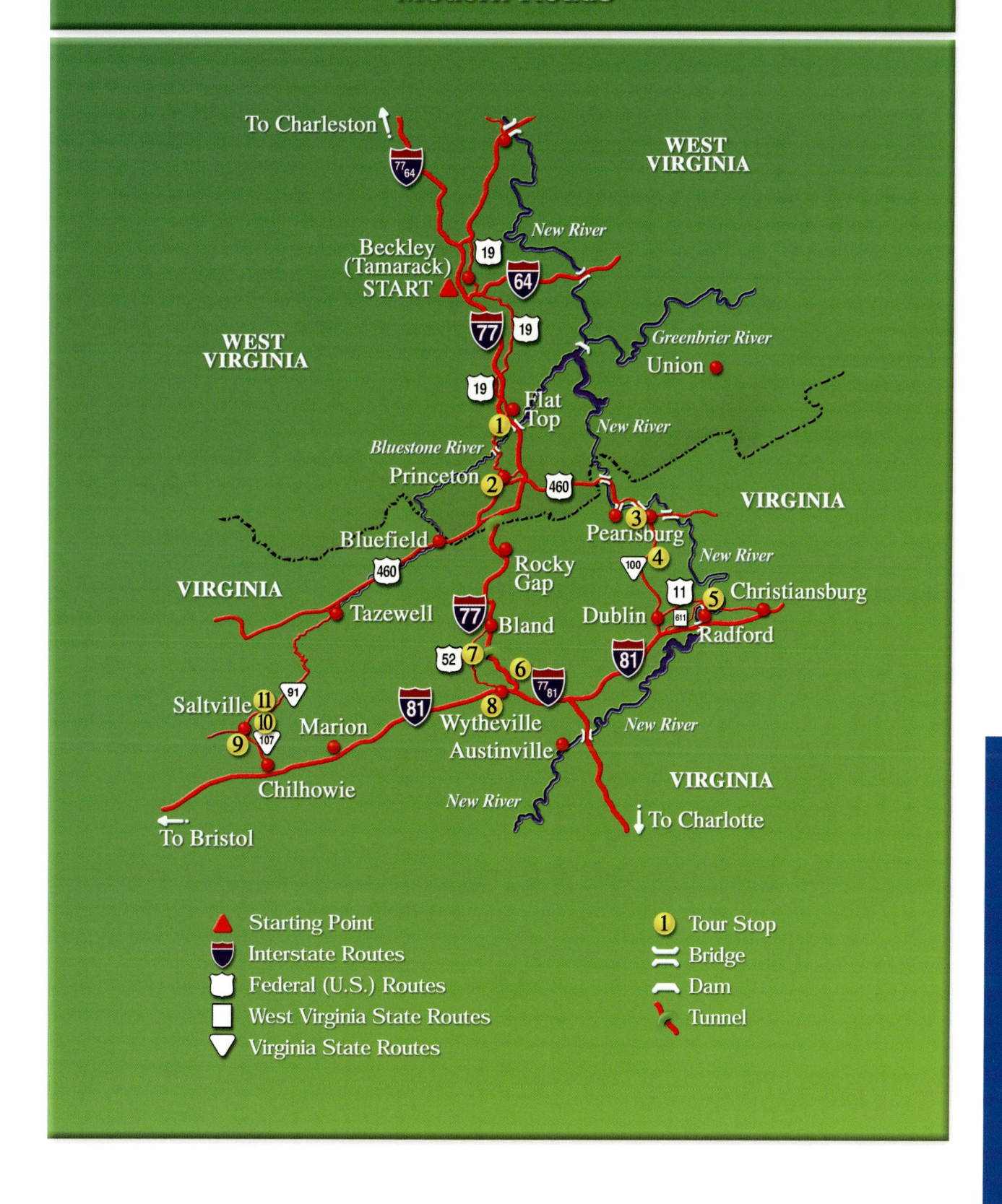

Geography of the New River

The New River begins in the mountains of western North Carolina, flows some 250 miles going northeast into western Virginia, then turns northwest through "The Narrows" into West Virginia. After entering West Virginia, the River pushes through the Allegheny Mountains carving out the 65-mile New River Gorge from Hinton to Gauley Bridge. At the northern end of the Gorge, the New River, is joined by the Gauley River, forming the Kanawha River, which flows another 90 miles west to the Ohio River. The River was discovered in the 1670s by English explorers seeking furs and a passage to the Western Ocean. While named the New River, ironically geologists suggest that it is one of the oldest rivers in North America. The river was flowing northwest before the uplift of the Appalachian Mountains, creating the Gorge. The Gorge at the northern (lower) end of the river passes through steep mountains. At the southern (upper) end the river passes through the open valley in Virginia. All of the New River Valley provided difficult terrain for military operations of the Civil War.

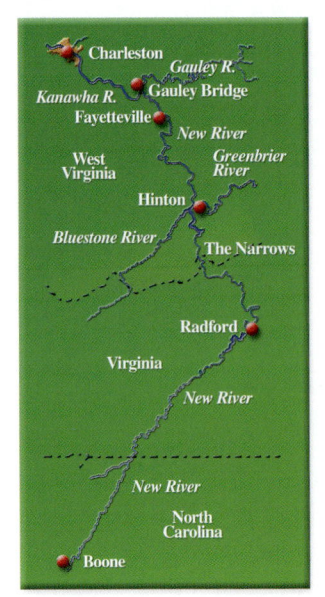

Overview of Day Three

The **Day One Tour** covered the fighting in 1861 and 1862 to control Gauley Bridge and the pathway between the New and Kanawha River Valleys. The tour visited sites of battles and skirmishes including Hawks Nest, Gauley Bridge, Cotton Hill, Kessler's Cross Lane, Carnifex Ferry, Sewell Mountain, and Fayetteville.

The **Day Two Tour** examined the struggles along the northeastern side of the New River Valley to control the James River & Kanawha Turnpike and the Greenbrier Valley. Union forces attempted to push through the mountains to destroy the railroad targets and bridge over the New River. Both sides launched raids and experimented with finding appropriate size and composition of their forces for effective operations. The tour visited the sites of Lee's Headquarters at Meadow Bluff, the raids of 1862-1863, Tuckwiller Hill, Battle of Lewisburg, Battle of White Sulphur Springs, Webster's Raid at Huntersville, and the Battle of Droop Mountain.

The **Day Three Tour** takes you to sites where Union and Confederate forces met in 1862, 1863, and 1864 to gain control of the southwestern side of the New River, south along the Raleigh & Grayson Turnpike from Gauley Bridge to Fayetteville, Raleigh Court House (Beckley), to Princeton, through Stoney Gap on to Wytheville and Grayson County, Virginia.

THE CIVIL WAR IN THE NEW RIVER VALLEY

The Union forces finally found the right composition of force to take them successfully to the three objectives – railroad bridge, lead mines, salt works. The Tour describes the routes to travel and nine sites to visit. Maps and narratives will explain both the events leading to the sites, as well as what to look for at each site. Maps show the modern road network as well as the historic route for the tour.

The **Day Three** driving tour is approximately 205 miles – one way – from Tamarack to Saltville. Several options are offered at the end of the trip, for the return to Tamarack, in Beckley. Each option adds about 105 miles – but the driving time varies considerably. Driving time – tour time – time out for lunch, *etc.,* for the one-way tour is about nine hours. The quick return adds 1 1/2 hours, the slower routes 2 1/2 hours. This is a long day tour. You may want to do it in segments.

The drive from Beckley to Princeton adds 45 minutes each way. If you start in Princeton, you can read the introductory material, and **Stop #1** before you start. Much of the route for the Day Three Tour is on interstate highway, and between large towns, so there are plenty of places for food and gas. There is a sandwich shop on Walker Mountain. Saltville has two small restaurants – no "fast food."

In each section, it is important to read all the driving instructions **before** you drive that section.

In both text and maps, names, units, and placement that are in blue are Union; those in red are Confederate.

There are **eleven** Stops on the **Day Three Tour.**

Stop #1 – Clark House Skirmish
   Flat Top/Bluestone – May 1, 1862
Stop #2 – Battle of Pigeon Roost
   Princeton – May 16-17, 1862
Stop #3 – Battle of Giles Court House
   Pearisburg, Va. – May 10, 1862
Stop #4 – Battle of Cloyd's Mountain
   May 9, 1864
      #4a – Union approach
      #4b – Confederate line
      #4c – Cleburne Wayside –
         pursuit and aftermath
Stop #5 – New River –Railroad Bridge
   Central Depot – Radford
Stop #6 – Cove Mountain Battle
   May 10, 1864
Stop #7 – Toland's Raid
   Big Walker Mountain lookout –
   July 13-21, 1863
Stop #8 – Battle of Wytheville
   July 18, 1863
Stop #9 – Overlook for Saltville
      Campaign
   Oct. – Dec. 1864
Stop #10 – First Battle for Saltville
   October 2, 1864
      #10a – Chestnut Ridge
      #10b – Elizabeth Hill
         Cemetery
      #10c – Allison Gap
Stop #11 – The Second Battle for
      Saltville – Stoneman's Raids
   Dec. 1864-March 1865

Chronology for Third Day Tour

The Stops on the tour do not follow in strict chronological order. That would require much doubling back and zigzagging. The following chronology may be referred to at any point of the tour.

April–May 1862–Gen. Jacob Cox conducts an offensive to destroy the railroad bridge at Central Depot (Radford). He uses the Raleigh-Grayson Turnpike on the southwest side of the New River, and sends a feint attack along the James & Kanawha Turnpike.

May 1, 1862–Skirmish at Clark House (Stop #1)

May 10, 1862–Battle at Giles Court House (Stop #3)

May 16-17, 1862–Battle of Pigeon Roost – Princeton, W.Va. (Stop #2) Cox falls back to Flat Top Mountain

May 23, 1862–Feint on James River & Kanawha Turnpike results in the **Battle of Lewisburg** (See Day Two Tour)

August–December 1862 Raids by both sides occur (See Day Two Tour)

Jan. – May 1863 Raids continue (See Day Two Tour)

June – July 1863 Troops withdraw from the New River Theater for the Gettysburg and Vicksburg campaigns

July 13–21, 1863 Toland's Raid to Wytheville. (Stops #7 & #8)

Aug.– Dec. 1863 Averell conducts three raids: White Sulphur Springs, Droop Mountain, Salem. (See Day Two Tour.)

May 1864–General Crook and General Averell advance as part of General Grant's combined offensive.

May 9, 1864–Battle of Cloyd's Mountain (Stops #4a, b, c).

May 10, 1864–Crook burns Railroad Bridge at Central Depot. (Stop #5)

May 10, 1864 –Battle at Cove Mountain (Stop #6)

Oct.-Dec. 1864–Battles of Saltville (Stops #9, 10, & 11)

The **Day Three Tour** begins at the Visitors Center at **Tamarack**, located at Exit 45 on the West Virginia Turnpike– Interstate 77/64, in Beckley, West Virginia. The tour is 205 miles in length, ending in Saltville, Virginia. Unlike the Day One and Day Two Tours, this is a one-way tour.

At the end of the tour, there are several options for returning to Tamarack – adding about 105 miles to the trip. Instructions include distances between turns and stops. The symbol **(TM-00)** indicates the total miles traveled to that point. In most cases mileage is "rounded off" to the nearest mile.

Odometers may vary considerably so the mileage indicated may not match yours, but by carefully following directions, and using the maps, you should not get very lost. Don't hesitate to ask local residents for directions.

You should read all driving directions in each travel section before starting that section, because the directions may also contain things to look for as you go between "Stops." At each "Stop" read the information and then explore the area as suggested. Be respectful of private property at some "Stops."

> **On the first leg of the tour you will travel 26 miles to Stop #1. Proceed from Tamarack going south on Interstate 77 toward Bluefield for 5.8 miles. I-64 East is the same as I-77 South. When I-64 turns off, be sure you stay on the right hand side. Stay on I-77 South toward Bluefield.**
>
> A few miles after the Toll Booths ($1.25 for cars) just past mile marker 27, you will start to go over the top of Flat Top Mountain. Look for the elevation sign (3,252 ft.). Just to the right of the roadway is the location of "Camp Jones," where the Union forces established a base for their 1862 advance.

View from the top of Flat Top Mountain looking south

As you start down Flat Top at mile marker 26 you will view much of the theater of the southwest side of the New River Valley campaign. As you go down the mountain, you can see the view that General Jacob Cox described in 1862. (See Map 30.)

"Looking south from Flat-top Mountain we see the basin of the Blue-stone River, which flows northeastward into New River. This basin, with that of the Greenbrier on the other side of the New River, forms the broadest stretch of cultivated land found between the mountain ranges, though the whole country is rough and broken even here. The crest of Flat-top Mountain curves southward around the headwaters of the Blue-stone, and joins the more regular ranges in Tazewell County. The straight ridge of East-River Mountain forms a barrier on the southern side of the basin, more than thirty miles from the summit of Flat-top where Scammon's camp was placed on the road from Raleigh C. H. to Princeton, the county-seat of Mercer. The Narrows of New River where that streams breaks through the mountain barrier I have described, and the road from Princeton to Giles C. H. passes through the defile.

"Only one other outlet from the basin goes southward, and that is where the road from Princeton to Wytheville passes through Rocky Gap, a gorge of the wildest character, some thirty miles westward from the Narrows. These passes were held by Confederate forces, whilst their cavalry, under Colonel W. H. Jenifer, occupied Princeton and presented a skirmishing resistance to our advance-guard."

That "Skirmish" was at the **Clark House,** about four miles farther down the mountain. The building of the modern road, I-77, destroyed the location of the Clark House, and there is no safe place to stop. The Clark House was just to the left of the road at mile marker 22. <u>You will be going down a very steep hill with a dangerous curve at the bottom mile, mile marker 21. Be careful.</u> **Just after you pass mile marker 19, turn right into the "Rest Area–Scenic View." Go through the rest area "Car" parking lot as if you were exiting the lot. Turn right into the "Scenic Overlook." Go 0.5 mile to the parking area. The gate to the overlook may be closed during winter and is always closed from dusk to dawn.** The overlook to the right shows the difficult broken terrain of the gorge of the Bluestone River. The overlook to the left looks at the bridge that was named in honor of a soldier killed in the Korean War. Enjoy the view. If the weather is appropriate, you may want to sit at one of the benches to read about the *Skirmish at the Clark House.* **Stop #1**

The Bluestone Gorge

Stop #1 – The Clark House Skirmish – May 1, 1862

Union forces under the command of General William Rosecrans had gained control of the lower New River in the summer and fall of 1861 (Day One Tour). During the winter, Rosecrans had gotten a plan approved to advance south, with the objective of taking the Railroad Bridge and marching toward Knoxville to "liberate" eastern Tennessee.

Rosecrans was transferred to Tennessee, and his replacement as commander of the Mountain Dept., General John Freemont, decided to continue the plan. General Jacob Cox was given the task of a traditional combined arms attack (infantry, cavalry, artillery) to invade the upper New River and cut the Tennessee & Central Virginia Railroad at the bridge over the New River. Cox would act as a feint on the other side of the New River.

The main force of two brigades, Col. E. P. Scammon – 12th Ohio Infantry, 23rd Ohio Infantry, 30th Ohio Infantry, McMullen's Battery, 2nd (West) Va. Cavalry, and Col. Augustus Moor's 28th Ohio Infantry, 34th Ohio Infantry, 37th Ohio Infantry, Simmond's Battery, Smith's Ohio Cavalry, plus **250 wagons,** began the move south from Fayetteville in April but was delayed by rain swollen streams.

The Union force moved ponderously slowly with all the wagons and taking time putting up a telegraph line for communications. Cox had cautiously ordered his commanders not to move ahead of their supplies. They were spread over miles of road.

THE CIVIL WAR IN THE NEW RIVER VALLEY

Map 30: Union Advance on Clark House
May 1, 1862

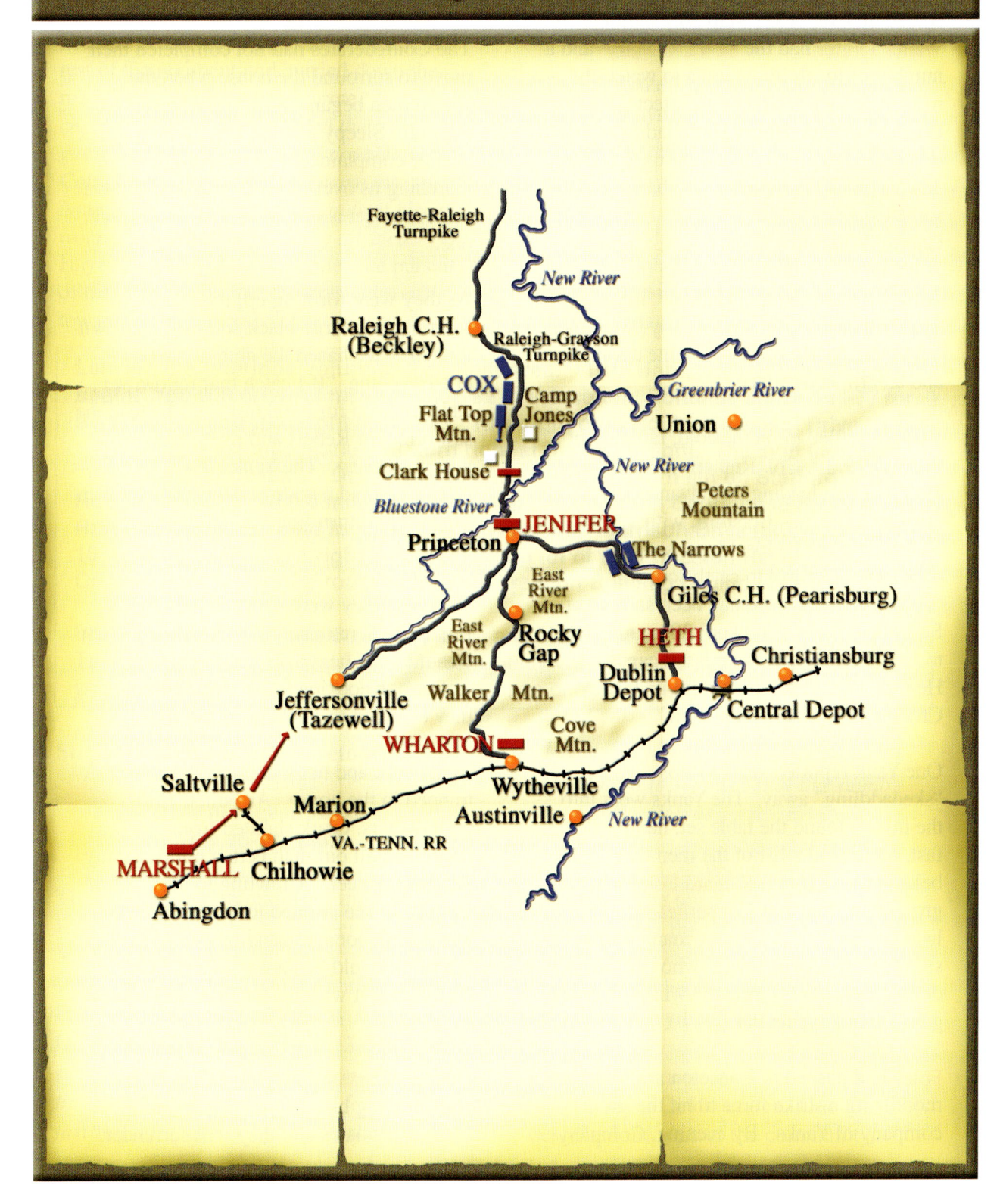

Map 31: Driving Tour • Modern Princeton
Showing Stop #2 of Day Three Tour

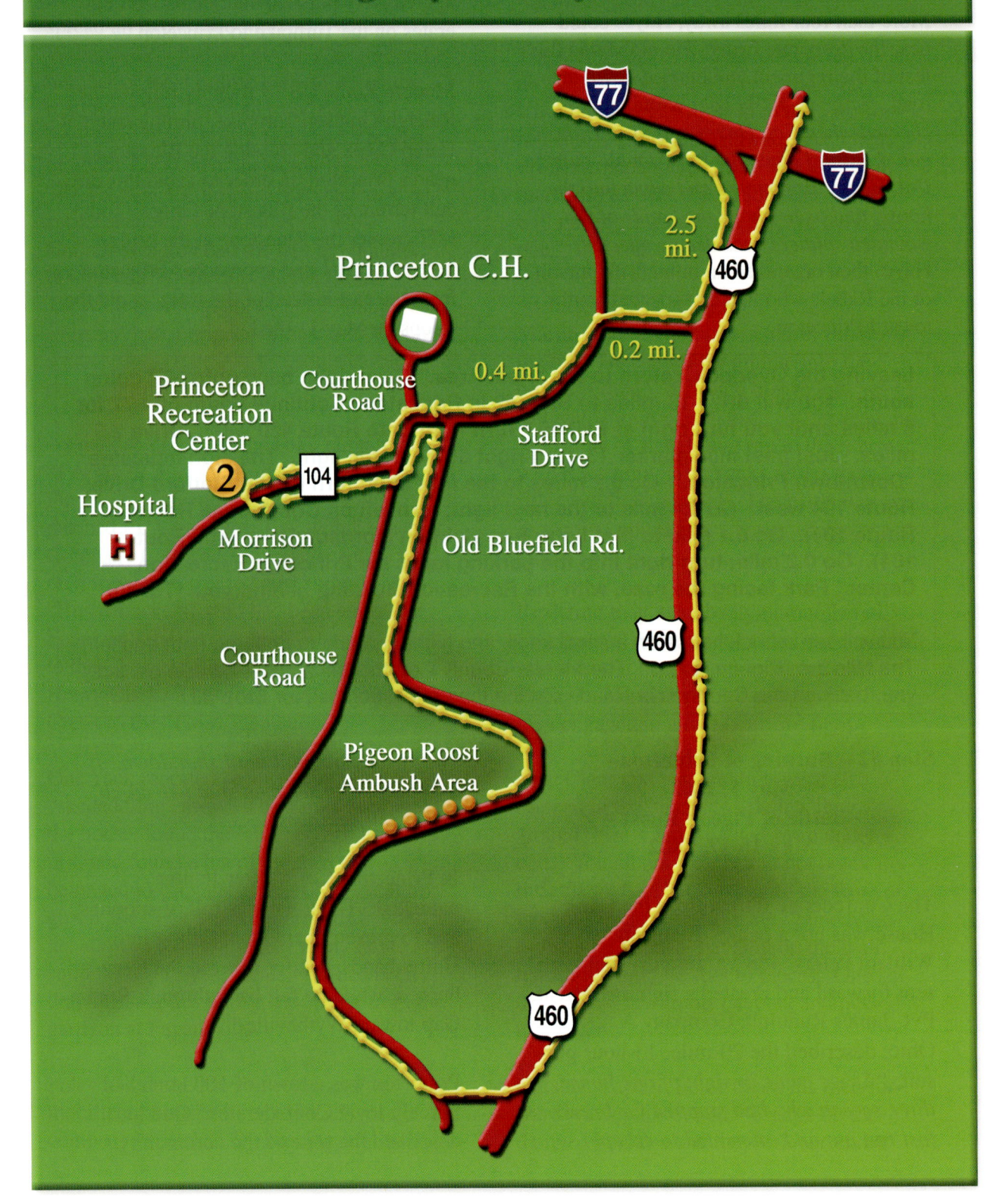

THE CIVIL WAR IN THE NEW RIVER VALLEY 95

Movements
May 15, 1862

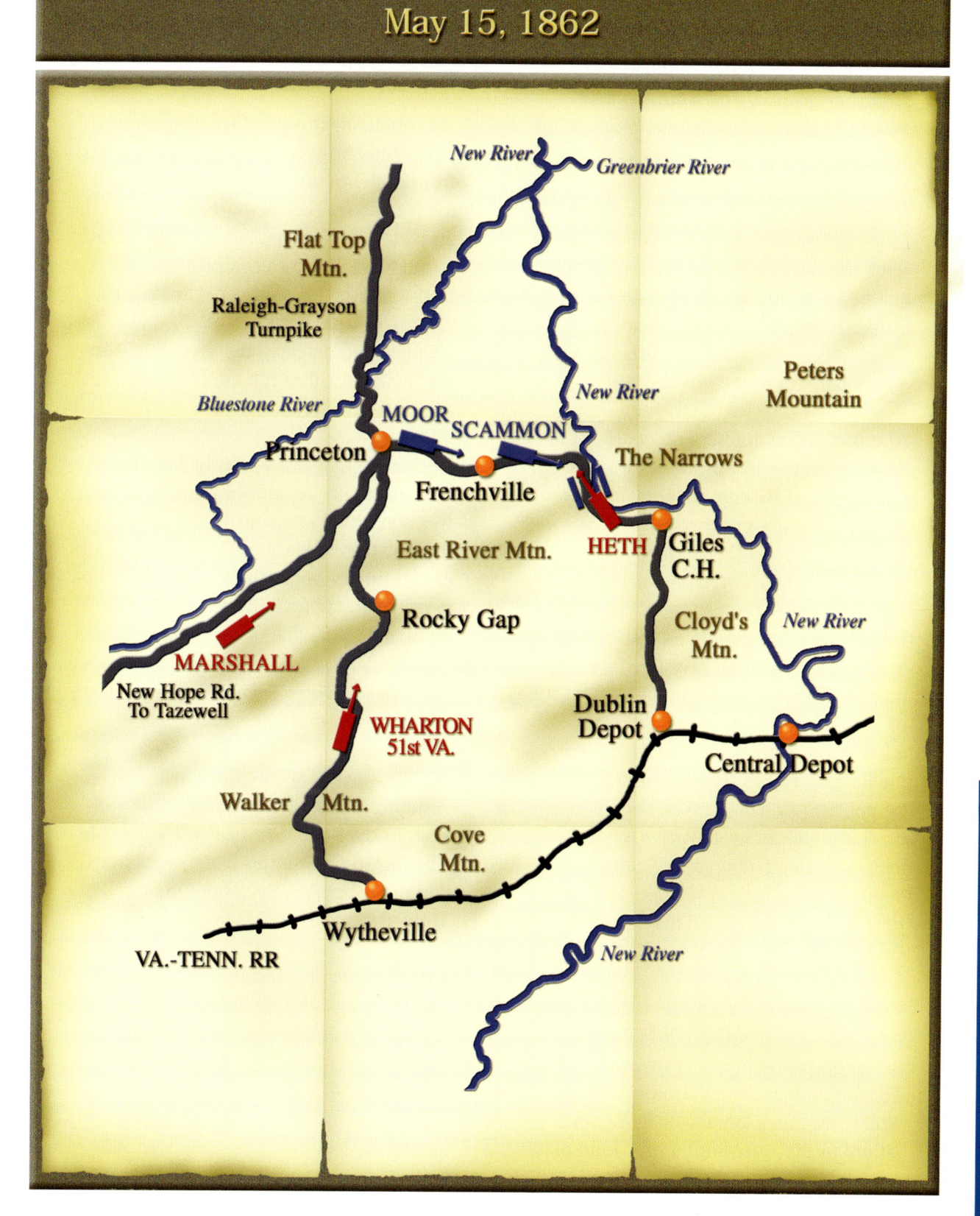

Map 32

New River
Greenbrier River

Flat Top Mtn.

Raleigh-Grayson Turnpike

Bluestone River
New River

Peters Mountain

MOOR SCAMMON
Princeton The Narrows
Frenchville

East River Mtn. HETH
Giles C.H.

Rocky Gap Cloyd's Mtn.
New River

MARSHALL

New Hope Rd. To Tazewell

WHARTON 51st VA. Dublin Depot

Central Depot

Walker Mtn.

Cove Mtn.

Wytheville
VA.-TENN. RR

New River

"Mercer's farmers and their wives gathered in Princeton each Saturday, bringing with them wagons, and on horseback, butter, eggs, bacon, and other goods, wares and merchandise. The men sat around on rail fences, good boxes, gathered in groups here and there, whittling and chewing homemade tobacco, and cussing the yankees."

When told to burn the town, they did! Judge Alexander Mahood torched his splendid home so quickly, it was reported that he neglected to untie his dog from inside the burning inferno. The Courthouse itself went up in flames with only a handful of records rescued.

At dusk, as Union forces approached, all the town was in flames. Pvt. Rudulph recorded, *"As we came in sight of the town we could see the smoke rooling up over the treetops. Why are they so foolhardy. Surely they are a stiff necked people."*

Union forces tried to douse the flames, but were only able to save five or six homes. The town was gone in ashes, one of the rare instances in the Civil War where Confederates burned their own town. Col. Hayes recorded in his diary, *"A good day's work."* Another soldier of the 23rd Ohio wrote, *"What a day…fun for us but terrible fright, destruction and death to the people of this quiet valley."* Pvt. Rudulph concluded his account, *"This was a hard day's work."*

Col. Jenifer was harshly criticized, but may have made the best decision. The "scorched earth policy" proved effective. The Union was denied a supply base, which became a key factor in the final failure of the 1862 "full army" kind of advance which was so dependent on continuous supply. Col. Hayes was praised for his good work, but also cautioned by his brigade commander, Col. Scammon, not to advance so precipitously that he would outrun his supply.

During the next week, Gen. Cox slowly pushed his brigades forward on the roads from Flat Top through Princeton toward the Narrows. The forward elements of the army, once again the 23rd Ohio, had gone through the Narrows and occupied Giles Court House (Pearisburg). On May 10, 1862, General Henry Heth's Brigade attacked and defeated the 23rd Ohio, forcing them back through the Narrows. (See Stop #3.)

During the first two weeks of May, Cox continued to bring his army forward, but was concerned about his lengthy supply line and the evidence of Confederates gathering south of him. The Regimental history of the 30th Ohio indicated the supply problem, saying that in early May, *"For eight days the allowance of rations was one cracker, with a small quantity of sugar, coffee, beans, and rice, to each man."*

A slow moving army of occupation, stringing wires, and being supplied with wagons over one dirt road was in trouble when nearly 100 miles from steam transportation supply. (See **Day One Tour**–Role of Steam Transportation.)

The Confederates responded to the invasion. General Humphry Marshall, newly appointed to command the Army of Southwest Virginia, tried to coordinate an attack by forces from three directions. Gen. Marshall was an imposing man, almost six feet tall, weighing over 300 pounds. His difficulty riding a horse made him less than well suited for campaigning in the mountains. There were fears he would be an easy target for snipers. He said that he would surround himself with fat staff officers. He struggled and disagreed with nearly all his fellow officers, writing longer reports than any other Confederate General, usually directly to Jefferson Davis or Lee, bypassing the chain of command.

Marshall ordered an encirclement and coordinated attack on Princeton for May 16. Heth was to come from the Narrows, Wharton from Rocky Gap, and Marshall's force from Jeffersonville (Tazewell). The plan began to fall apart when Wharton sent a message that he could not arrive at Princeton before 9:00 a.m. on the 17th. No message came from Heth.

The Union commanders, without clear knowledge of the terrain or road networks, had become cautious after the skirmish at Giles Court House. Cox was also aware that Gen. McClellan's offensive on the Peninsula toward Richmond had bogged down, and "Stonewall" Jackson was on the offensive in the Shenandoah.

Growing concerned with a coordinated Confederate attack, he sent his two brigades forward toward the Narrows, hoping to hit Heth before Marshall could arrive. He also sent the 37th Ohio over East River Mountain on a narrow trail to scout the Confederate approach on the Turnpike from Wytheville. On May 16, Cox was in Princeton with a small Headquarters force. (See Map 32.)

On May 16, 1862, contact was first made in mid-afternoon as Marshall's force skirmished with a detachment of 1st Ohio Cavalry four miles west of Princeton, on the New Hope Road from Tazewell.

Pvt. Robert King, 54th Va. Infantry, wrote in his inimitable style and spelling, *"...we arrived within gun shot of the enemy about 3 oclock ... we fought then for fore miles slaying them on every hand...arived within 3 or 4 hundred yards of the cort house in crossing a fence one of our men fired his gun by accident which prevented us from sorounding them [as] the yankeeys pored forth a very sever fire...."*

At 5:00 p.m. Cox sent messages for his forward brigades to turn back and concentrate on Princeton. The Confederates deployed on the New Hope Road were pushing toward town; but aware that Wharton would not be up until the next morning, Marshall decided not to attack, but rather spread out onto the brush and wood covered hill, south of town–Pigeon Roost. Pvt. King wrote, *"we took supper in prinston we ate crackers and molasses till we coldent rest lay under arms al night...."*

As night fell, Cox, still with only his HQ force of less than 1,000, nervously facing the Confederates with more than 2,000, decided to evacuate the town going to his main force near Frenchville. By 10:00 p.m. a Confederate patrol found the town deserted. Marshall still hoped that Heth would block the Union escape, and with Wharton arriving in the morning he could hit the Federals from all sides.

Before nightfall, Wharton, with his 800 men of the 51st Va., had reached Rocky Gap, while Colonel L. von Blessingh and his German 37th Ohio, after having gone over East River Mountain, were camped only four miles away, behind the Confederates. During the night, Cox, with his two brigades, decided to turn back to Princeton to face the Confederates.

By dawn, Union forces were moving back into the burned out town in full sight of the Confederates hidden up on the wooded hills. By 6:00 a.m. both sides had taken position and had begun cannon fire and skirmishing. Both commanders were waiting for their full force to arrive. Both thought they were outnumbered, and hoped the other would attack.

At first light, Wharton began his march from Rocky Gap, leaving in his rear a medical wagon with a barrel of whiskey. Without knowledge of what was in front of them, the 37th Ohio was also marching north on the Turnpike heading for Princeton. Finding the barrel of whiskey, the soldiers imbibed, brightening up the morning march, which proceeded with boisterous song.

As Wharton arrived at Princeton, the light skirmishing quieted down. The 51st Va. took a position on a high spur of ground on the Confederate right, where the road took a hard turn between the hills. At about 10:00 a.m. Col. von Blessingh's 37th Ohio began to loudly approach the long curve in the road at Pigeon Roost. The 51st Va. turned about, went quietly down the hill, and took position in high grass behind a fence along the road.

The Germans walked into the trap. The Confederate fire left 14 killed and 46 wounded. Over the hill, in Princeton, the sounds of the fight were heard. The 28th Ohio was ordered forward, but for some unknown reason, the order "was not complied with." Col. von Blessingh was in a trap and no help was coming. He decided to fall back, cut across country and get back to Union lines. (He came out about where Route 460 intersects with I-77.) Confederates pursued the retreating Germans.

Adjutant Peter Otey jumped the fence and found himself confronting a dazed Union soldier with his rifle raised in firing position. Otey fired a warning shot at the soldier's feet and took him prisoner, asking him why he had not fired his rifle. The response was, "Well, Mister my gun ain't loaded."

Both forces spent the rest of the day looking at each other. Where was Heth? He had advanced to about five miles east of Princeton, but then halted, turned around and went back to the Narrows. Some mysterious courier (never identified) had told Heth that the Confederates had been defeated and were retreating south. Heth did not bother to check the report. During the night, Cox decided to fall back to Flat Top. The Confederates did not pursue. The battle and the campaign were over.

Aftermath –
There was plenty of criticism and praise on both sides. General Cox, who had started with such ambitious hopes, was thoroughly disheartened with the New River theater. He said, *"Our movements have been valuable as a reconnaissance … [but] … the character of this mountain country and the net-work of roads…is such that no advance movements can be made with entire security to the line of communication without leaving strong detachments at important posts along the line."* This would have required a size of force he didn't have and could not sustain.

THE CIVIL WAR IN THE NEW RIVER VALLEY

Battle of Princeton • "Pigeon Roost"
May 16 - 17, 1862

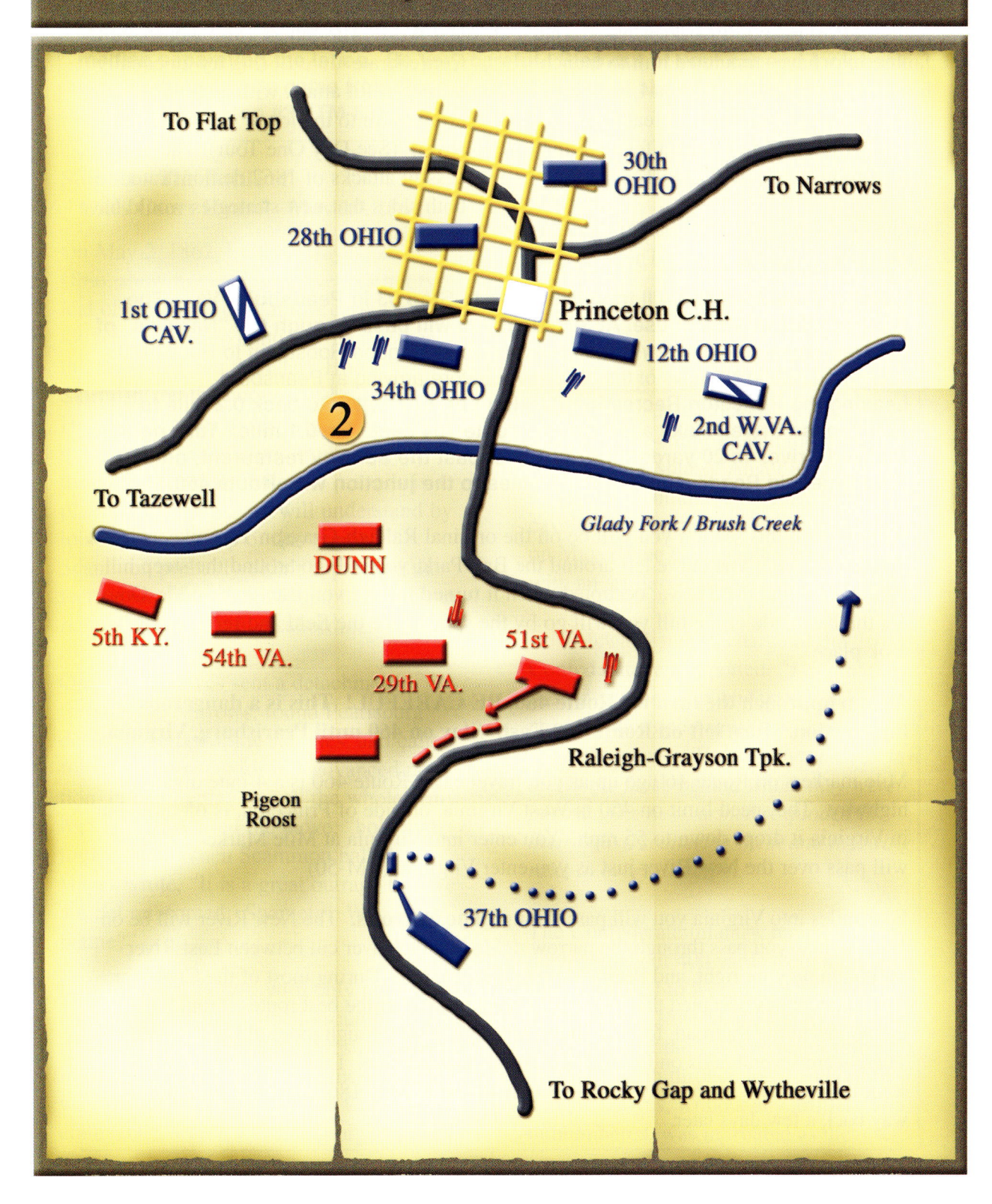

Map 33

To Flat Top
30th OHIO
To Narrows
28th OHIO
1st OHIO CAV.
Princeton C.H.
34th OHIO
12th OHIO
2nd W.VA. CAV.
②
To Tazewell
Glady Fork / Brush Creek
DUNN
5th KY.
54th VA.
29th VA.
51st VA.
Raleigh-Grayson Tpk.
Pigeon Roost
37th OHIO
To Rocky Gap and Wytheville

Battle of Giles Court House
May 10, 1862

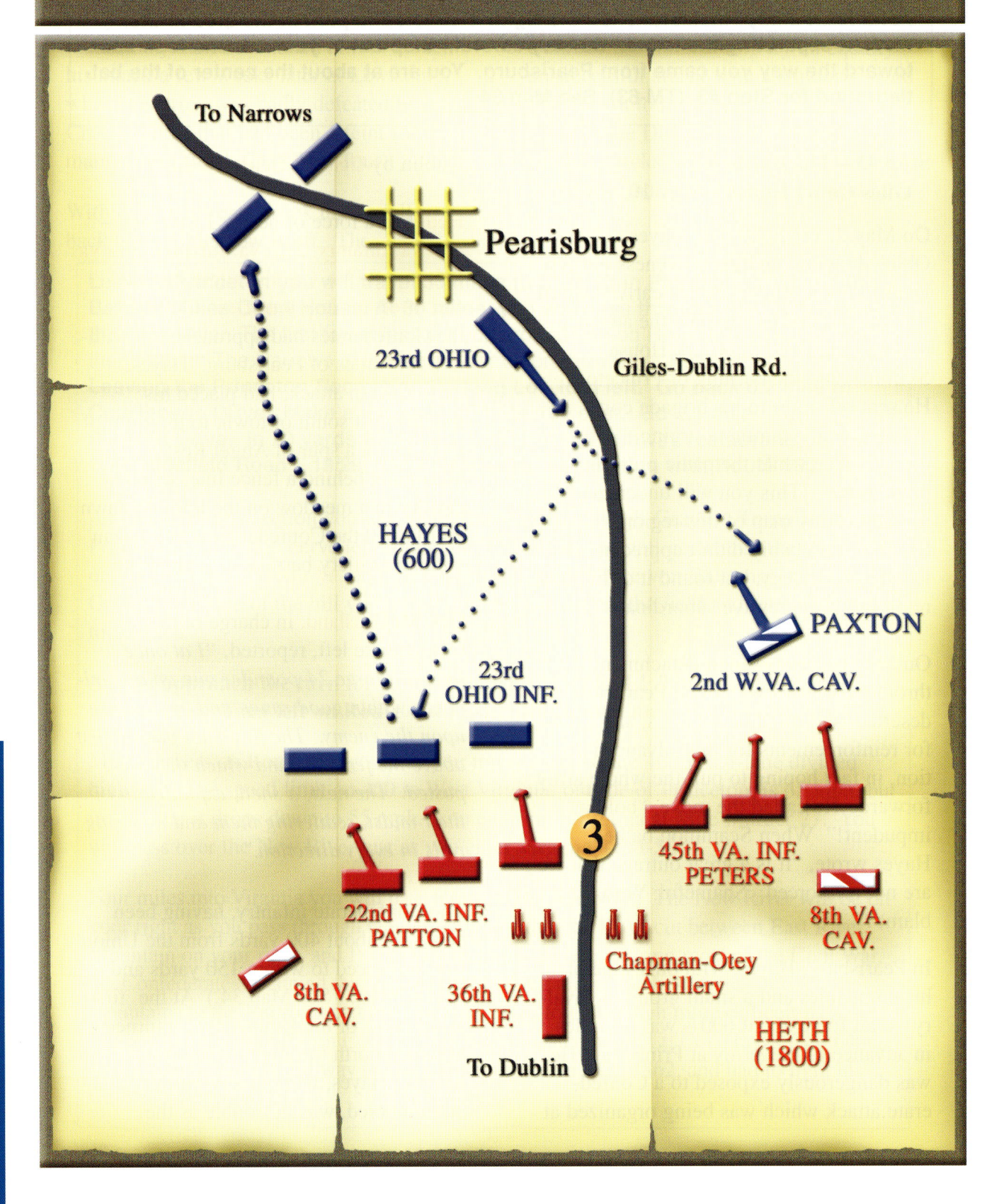

Map 34

To Narrows

Pearisburg

23rd OHIO

Giles-Dublin Rd.

HAYES (600)

23rd OHIO INF.

PAXTON
2nd W.VA. CAV.

3

22nd VA. INF.
PATTON

45th VA. INF.
PETERS

8th VA. CAV.

8th VA. CAV.

36th VA. INF.

Chapman-Otey Artillery

HETH (1800)

To Dublin

THE CIVIL WAR IN THE NEW RIVER VALLEY

Confederates began to work around his flanks.

Hayes tried to steady his men, "It's all right, boys, it's all right. We will fall back on something before night so that we can give them hell." He slowly fell back to a position just north of town where he made a brief stand. The Confederates pushed forward again. Colonel George Patton, leading his 22nd Va., was hit. The bullet hit a $20 gold piece that Patton had put in his belt, which deflected the bullet. It was a nasty looking wound, but not dangerous. He later went home to recuperate and missed the next battle at Lewisburg.

Under pressure, the Yanks now broke in a rout and fled for safe passage through the Narrows. They tried to burn the bridge over Wolf Creek, just before the Narrows. Pvt. Albert Singleton, 22nd Va., "ran a gauntlet of bullets from the Yankees, knocked down the burning brands of the bridge, and saved it from destruction." When the Yanks tried to make another stand in the Narrows, Heth sent some artillery across the river to high ground, and shelled the defenders. During this fire Hayes was slightly wounded by a shell fragment above his knee. The Yanks then fell back to where East River flows into the New River.

They had retreated 7 miles but were now safe. Union casualties were 20 killed, 50 wounded. The Confederates lost 2 killed, 4 wounded. The Confederates had won a nice victory. Hayes had been impetuous, but showed real promise as a fighter. The victorious Confederates occupied Pearisburg and established a base called "Camp Success." General Marshall began to plan the attack on Princeton that we examined at stop #2.

The Battles at Giles Court House and Princeton had ended the Union advance of the spring of 1862. During the fall of 1862, and throughout 1863, the Union commanders would experiment with **Raids** to accomplish their objectives of destroying the railroad bridge, lead mines, and salt works. We will see one of these raids–Toland's–at **Stop #7**.

In 1864, the Union launched a major offensive to destroy the Railroad bridge. General George Crook led that force to Cloyd's Mountain, a battle that we will examine next at **Stop #4**.

Continue South on Route 100. You will drive about 13 miles to Stop #4a on Cloyd's Mountain. After going about nine miles, Route 42 will intersect from the right. This is the road that General Crook used to come from Rocky Gap up to Cloyd's Mountain. **Stay on Route 100.**
On the night of May 8, 1864, the Union Army was camped along the next 2 miles of the road, by Big Walker Creek, to the pass where the road cuts through Big Walker Mountain.
Drive along the creek through the pass. Continue on Rt. 100; drive along the creek through the pass of Big Walker Mountain (mile 10.5). Route 100, a new 4-lane road, goes up Cloyd's Mountain passing over the top of the mountain at 12 miles. This is the route Crook took on the morning of the battle. **SLOW DOWN.** Stay in the left lane. At 12.8 miles pull off left in the median and stop by the Historic Road Marker, "The Battle of Cloyd's Mountain." Stop #4A.

THE CIVIL WAR IN THE NEW RIVER VALLEY

At Stop #4a look at Map #35 for the routes that Crook and Averell used to approach the target of the Raid, the Railroad Bridge at Central Depot. Look at Map #36. Stop #4a is Crook's Location at the outset of the battle. The Confederates were located on the bluff about a mile in front of this position – (Stop #4b). Read the material for Stop #4a. Look at Map #37. **When you leave Stop #4a, you will cross the bridge over Back Creek and go up the hill to the Confederate position, Stop #4b. Look at the photograph.**

Stop #4a – The Battle of Cloyd's Mountain–Approaches and Union Position – May 9, 1864

In 1862, using established supply lines, General Jacob Cox's army failed to destroy the New River Railroad Bridge at Central Depot. The Union tried different modes of attack in 1863, the raids. We will look at one of the raids (Toland's) at Stops #7 and #8. The Union commanders learned lessons from all of the raids (See Averell's Raids–Day Two Tour), that were later put to use in the Spring of 1864.

After three years of frustration, Lincoln's armies had won victories in the summer and fall of 1863 – Gettysburg, Vicksburg, Chattanooga. In January 1864, Lincoln promoted U. S. Grant to the rank of Lieutenant General and called him to Washington to take command of all forces and to coordinate the attacks on the Confederacy.

Grant planned an offensive for May 1864. All forces would attack at many points to prevent the Confederacy from shifting resources from one theater to another. Grant's strategy was if a General *"can't skin himself he can hold a leg while some one else skins."*

THE CIVIL WAR IN THE NEW RIVER VALLEY

Map 35

Averell's and Crook's Routes
May 1864

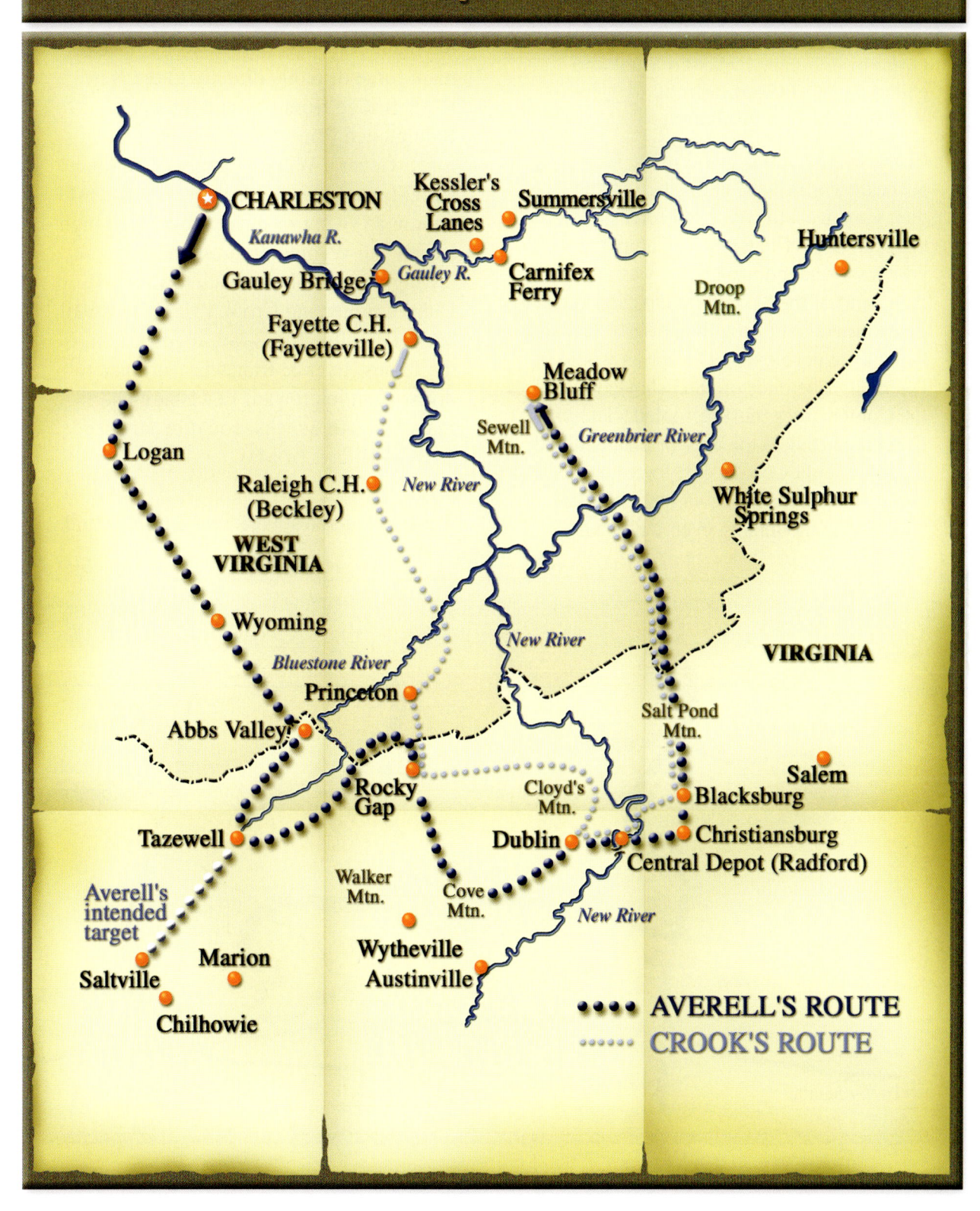

- Charleston
- Kanawha R.
- Kessler's Cross Lanes
- Summersville
- Gauley Bridge
- Gauley R.
- Carnifex Ferry
- Huntersville
- Fayette C.H. (Fayetteville)
- Droop Mtn.
- Meadow Bluff
- Sewell Mtn.
- Greenbrier River
- Logan
- Raleigh C.H. (Beckley)
- New River
- White Sulphur Springs
- WEST VIRGINIA
- Wyoming
- New River
- VIRGINIA
- Bluestone River
- Princeton
- Abbs Valley
- Salt Pond Mtn.
- Rocky Gap
- Cloyd's Mtn.
- Salem
- Blacksburg
- Tazewell
- Dublin
- Christiansburg
- Central Depot (Radford)
- Averell's intended target
- Walker Mtn.
- Cove Mtn.
- New River
- Saltville
- Marion
- Wytheville
- Austinville
- Chilhowie

●●●● **AVERELL'S ROUTE**
•••• **CROOK'S ROUTE**

As Grant planned his attacks in the East, he wanted to make sure there would be no shifting of forces, east or west. The crucial railroad bridge over the New River had to be destroyed. Fearful that General Franz Sigel, commander of the Army of West Virginia, might bungle the task, Grant in February bypassed Sigel and called General George Crook to Washington for consultation.

Crook had been successful in the New River theater in 1861 and 1862. He had then gone west to command forces in the Chickamauga–Chattanooga Campaigns and got Grant's attention. Crook was put in command of the "Kanawha Division" and given orders to destroy the bridge. Several plans were developed. Deception would be essential. The raids of 1863 showed that the Confederates must be fooled. The Confederates held the interior line, and with the railroad they could shift forces to block any point of advance down the Valley or through the mountains, even with badly outnumbered forces.

The plan called for Sigel to leave sufficient force to guard the B&O Railroad, then advance down the Shenandoah Valley with 6,000, making Staunton appear to be the main objective. Crook would take a main force of 6,000 directly to the New River Bridge from Fayetteville via Raleigh and Princeton. To mask that force, General William Averell would take a highly mobile, all-cavalry force of 2,000 on a wide swing from Charleston, through Logan and Wyoming, to raid Saltville, tearing up the railroad back toward Dublin, protecting Crook's flank. A small but very visible force would go east on the James River & Kanawha Turnpike to divert attention toward Lewisburg and Staunton. All attacks would be launched in the first days of May.

The Confederates were aware of potential

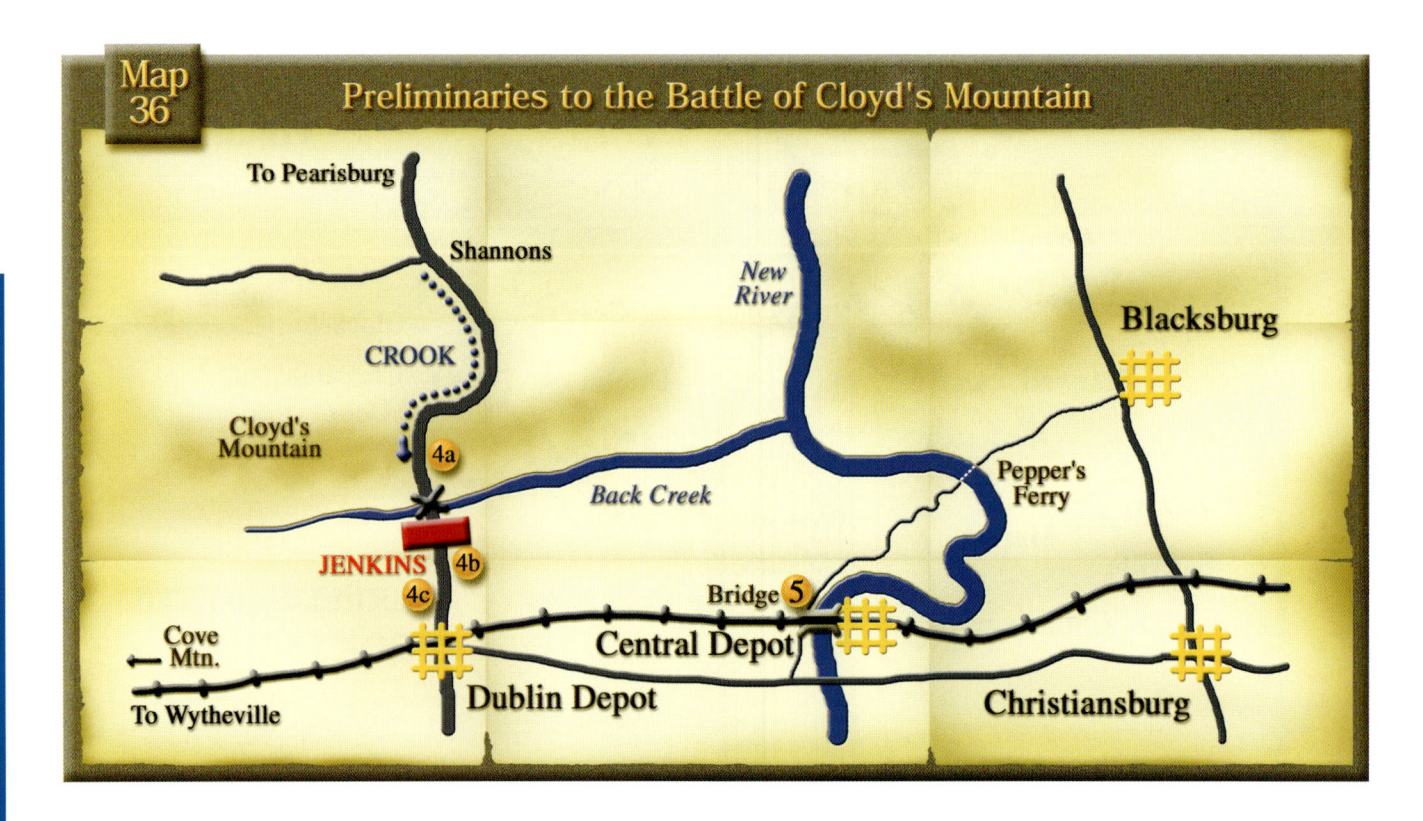

Map 36: Preliminaries to the Battle of Cloyd's Mountain

invasions. After the raids of 1863, a new commander was sent to The Army of Southwest Virginia, General John Breckenridge. He had been Vice-President of the United States before the war, and while he was a "political" general, he had shown some real skill. He had a difficult task. He was told by Davis and Lee that when the Union spring offensives began, he would not get any reinforcements. He would have to make do with 9,000 or so troops in his Department. If they were used correctly, they should be sufficient to ward off attack, as had happened for the last three years.

His force was spread out, covering the approaches used in the past. In the north, "Mudwall" Jackson covered the Huntersville–Greenbrier roads from Beverly. Echols covered the line from Lewisburg to Covington and Salem. McCausland's Brigade blocked the key roads in a fort built at Princeton. Wharton and "Grumble" Jones held the line from Tazewell to Saltville. The Saltville Garrison had the 45th Va. and 14 guns. In Abingdon, General John Hunt Morgan had a brigade of Kentucky cavalry. There were small garrisons at Dublin, Central Depot, and Wytheville. The Confederates could also use the railroad to move to any threatened point.

May 2, Crook began his advance, limiting each regiment to six wagons, no tents, each man carrying three days' rations. They had more than 140 miles to go. The 8th W. Va. Infantry and the "scouts" led by Lt. Richard Blazer went off toward Lewisburg with bands playing.

Confederate intelligence picked up the movement. Lee fell for the deception. He believed that the main effort would be at Staunton and ordered forces sent in that direction. Breckenridge responded to orders, and began to move McCausland, Echols, Wharton, and 12 guns (4,000 men) back to the railroad, heading for Staunton. General Albert Jenkins, recovering from a head wound received at Gettysburg, took command of the forces left in the Southwest Dept. (4,000 men, 12 guns). Before leaving, Breckenridge warned Jenkins, "You see the whole country west of New River is uncovered and depends on you."

The warm spring weather of April turned nasty on May 4, with an icy rain. The Union troops without tents tramped south, 17 miles the first day, then 21 and 23 miles. As the main column approached Princeton on May 6, they found the first Confederate pickets. Just a day earlier, McCausland's brigade had been withdrawn from the solid dirt fort that had been built at Princeton. As the Union forces approached, they were met by cavalry pickets who fired a shot or two and then fled to the west toward Tazewell, leaving the road south through Rocky Gap wide open.

Had McCausland's large brigade been entrenched in Princeton, Crook would have faced tough choices. He could have probably overwhelmed the garrison, but that would have meant a fight. In past raids, such a fight would likely have ended the raid well short of the objective. He could have by-passed the garrison, but that would have left a strong force in his rear to block any escape. Crook did not have to make these decisions, as McCausland was in Dublin getting ready to board trains for Staunton.

Not to be. In order to draw artillery fire away from his infantry, Crook ordered his two batteries, McMullen and Glassie, into action. **(Stop #4a.)**

At 11:00 a.m. an artillery duel began. White now in position heard the guns, thought it was the signal, and began his attack. The 14th W. Va. had never been in combat but surged forward to within 20 yards of the Confederate barricade firing volley after volley. They "could distinctly see a sheet of flames issuing from the Rebel works, but could not see a single Rebel, so completely were they protected by their defenses."

The 12th Ohio felt the same resistance. From the shooting, the dry leaves caught fire. One soldier wrote, "…the line slowly advanced with colors flying, through the burning woods, pouring in a steady fire." General Jenkins, riding his horse on the right, saw the danger to Beckley's 45th Va. Battalion and called for help from the 60th Va. and two artillery pieces. Under pressure, the Union attack subsided. The Yanks began to fall back. With a whoop the Rebels jumped over their barricade and began a counterattack. The Confederate right seemed secure.

On the Union right, Sickel's 3rd Brigade launched their attack in the open, and were under the heavy fire of Bryan's Battery and the 60th Va. Infantry on the bluff. All four Union regiments were stopped by the fire, with Col. R. H. Woolworth, 4th Pa., being killed by an artillery fragment hit to the groin. The 60th Va. let out a cheer, believing the battle was won.

In the center, Col. Hayes took his regiments across the nearly waist deep waters of Back Creek, telling them not to stop to fire, but to push to the base of the hill. General Crook, displaying his usual battlefield rashness, charged with these troops. He quickly ran into trouble as his boots filled with water. Captain Russell Hastings, 23rd Ohio, wrote, "The only objection he had to a corps commander leading a charge was that he had to be helped across the creek."

On the other side and under cover of the bluff, out of Confederate fire, Hayes realigned his men and was ready for a quick charge up the hill. His 23rd Ohio would meet their old rivals, the 45th Va. Infantry, which they had first met in 1861 at the Battle of Carnifex Ferry. The fight became a hand–to–hand combat. A member of the 23rd Ohio wrote, "We moved on rapidly right in front of the Rebble works under a mosgauing fire of musketry but our men did not flinch or faulter." They began to push through the thin Confederate line.

To the Confederate right, Beckley's small 45th Battalion, only 183 men, half without bayonets, were charging the fleeing Yanks. Col. White's second line was ready. The 9th W. Va. and 91st Ohio, hard fought veterans, were ordered to lie down, and let the retreating Yanks pass through. They then stood, fired into the Rebels, stopping them in their tracks. Now the movement was in the other direction, with the 9th and 91st charging up the hill and over the Confederate entrenchments. The battle had turned. It was about 11:30 a.m.

THE CIVIL WAR IN THE NEW RIVER VALLEY 111

> **Leaving Stop #4a, drive 0.9 mile. After crossing the bridge over Back Creek, drive up the hill to the second median cross-over. Find a safe place to park on the left at the median cross-over. Stop #4b.** You are now in the middle of the Confederate position. <u>After safely stepping out of your car, turn around facing back toward Cloyd's Mountain and Stop #4a.</u> Look at Map #37.
>
> Bryan's Battery & Co. A–36th Va. would have been on the high ground to your left. The 60th Va. would have been on the bluff just up and to your right. Sickel's first attack would have been along the line of the road you just drove. The land on either side of the road is private property. **Do not cross the fences.**

Stop #4b – Battle of Cloyd's Mountain – The Confederate line crumbles – May 9, 1864

General Jenkins on the Confederate right tried to stem the tide but was hit in the shoulder, a wound that would be fatal a few days later when a bandage was mishandled. Col. "Tiger John" McCausland, a 27-year-old, was now the Army commander. He sent the reserve 36th Va. to the right, and tried to turn Bryan's guns to the right. The guns could not fire effectively over the hill and over the intervening Confederates. The 36th Va. had to stop, and move back to face the onslaught from the right.

Back on the left Bryan's Battery was in trouble, with only one infantry company for protection. The 15th W. Va. had worked itself to the right of the hill, and was about to take the Confederate guns. The Union artillery, McMullen and Glassie, had come down the south slope of Cloyd's Mountain, and was hitting the Confederate infantry line with enfilade fire.

The fighting in the center and right flank was desperate. Before the battle, Capt. Russell Hastings, 23rd Ohio, had accused one of his long haired men of cowardice and told him to cut his hair. As that man now charged the hill, he shouted, "What do you think of long hair fighting now?"

Eighteen-year-old Pvt. John Kosht, 23rd Ohio, was the first to reach Lt. Hoge's gun in the center. He took off his cap and with an "Indian war whoop jammed it into the muzzle." The small unit of the Confederate Home Guard was overrun in the middle of the line. On this Sunday morning, a local minister, Reverend William Hickman, had left his congregation, and wearing civilian clothes and silk hat had joined the Guards. He was hit. Before dying, he urged, "Do your best boys, my work is done."

On the right flank, the fight of the 9th W. Va. to capture the flag of the 45th Va. left nine Yanks and 12 Rebels dead around the flag. Lt. Col. Edwin Harmon, 45th Va., waving his sword to rally his men, was fatally shot through his lungs. The Confederate right collapsed, falling back to a line with the retreating 36th Va. and 60th Va.

There was a brief "last stand" fight at the top of the hill (near the house you can see), but the onslaught could not be stopped. The Confederates broke into a run for Dublin. In less than an hour the bloody Battle of Cloyd's Mountain was over. The Union had lost 688 or nearly 10% of the force. The Confederates lost 538, almost 23% of their strength. Confederate officers were lost in large numbers, about 10% of the killed and wounded. They had fought fiercely to encourage their men. But the fighting was not over. There was a dash for Dublin. **(Stop #4c)**

> **Leaving Stop #4b, continue south on Route 100 for 2.5 miles. Turn right into "Cleburne Memorial Wayside Park" for Stop #4c.**
>
> The Wayside is a small park with a picnic bench, no facilities. See the Historical Marker and monument for Captain Christopher Cleburne, 2nd Ky. Cavalry, at the back left corner of the park.

Stop #4c – The Pursuit to Dublin – May 9–10, 1864

Crook realized the need to complete his victory and ordered his 400 cavalry to pursue. Some of the tired infantry, led by Hayes and Glassie's 1st Ky. battery, joined in the pursuit. A mile down the road, McCausland rounded up about 100 Confederates and set an ambush. The Union cavalry was surprised, but the approaching infantry had the Rebels on the run again until they hit a more formidable obstacle, Col. D. Howard Smith and 500 men of Morgan's 5th Ky. Cavalry, which had arrived by train at Dublin too late for the battle, but in time to act as a rear guard for the retreat. They met along the road, here by the "Wayside."

Again the Federal cavalry balked and turned away, leaving the advancing guns of Glassie's Yankee Kentuckians to face the Confederate dismounted Kentucky 5th Cavalry. The Rebel Kentuckians recognized the Union Kentuckians and attacked them, shouting, "Capture the renegade! Kill the damn southern Yankee!" Hayes rushed forward with some of the tired 23rd Ohio, telling the small number to "Yell like devils." One Ohio soldier wrote,

"One would have thought five thousand were in line instead of five hundred."

Capt. Cleburne was mortally wounded and requested to be buried where he fell. He was the brother of the famous Confederate, Major General Patrick Cleburne, killed later in Tennessee. The monument marks where he fell. The rear guard then fled for Dublin, but had bought more than an hour for the defeated Confederates to escape.

Cleburne Marker

At Dublin, McCausland turned east, hoping to make a stand to save the railroad bridge over the New River. (See Stop #5.) At 4:00 p.m. the advanced elements of Crook's tired army were entering Dublin. After four years of trying, the door to the strategic target was open. His men had gone 11 miles, fought a winning battle, and now, tired and hungry, enjoyed the supplies of Dublin. Hayes, exuberant, wrote, "This is our best fight." There was joy, but also sadness. In the camp near town that night, one soldier sadly lamented that there were "so many missing from our ranks."

THE CIVIL WAR IN THE NEW RIVER VALLEY

At the telegraph station, reading captured messages, Crook learned that Grant's advance on Richmond had bogged down and stopped in the Wilderness. He could find no mention of Gen. Sigel advancing up the Shenandoah Valley.

With Grant halted, the Confederates could send forces to trap Crook's intruding column. He had won a battle victory, but for any real success he had to get to the bridge as soon as possible.

Leaving Stop #4c, drive 10 miles to Stop #5 at the New River Bridge.

As you drive between Stop #4 and Stop #5, you will pass the outskirts of Dublin. When you turn onto Route 11 north, you will see the railroad tracks. You will drive along these tracks for seven miles. These are the tracks that Crook's men tore up on May 10, 1864. As you cross the New River Bridge, if you look to your right (upstream), you can see the modern railroad bridge, and the piles for the old bridge. Notice the hill on the east side of the bridge – where Radford High School is located – which was the location of the Confederate Batteries that will be described at Stop #5. After you turn around and re-cross the bridge, notice the high ground on the west side of the bridge and to the left, the position of the Union guns.

Continue south on Route 100 for two miles. Turn left on Route 11 north, going toward Radford. After 7.6 miles, you will cross the highway bridge over the New River. Stay in the left lane. At the light at the end of the bridge, turn left on Route 11 North. Turn left immediately at the red brick building, into the parking lot of the Radford Parks and Recreation Dept. This is a convenient place to turn around as you will be backtracking across the New River Bridge.

As you come out of the parking lot, turn right on Route 11 South. At the light, turn right to go back across the bridge. At the end of the bridge there is a flashing yellow light. Turn left on Route 626–Hazel Hollow Road. Drive 0.5 mile until you see the railroad bridge crossing over the road. SLOW DOWN. About 50 yards past the bridge turn left into a gravel pull-out. This is a boat access area. Park in the gravel area. Walk down to the river. Looking to your left, downstream, you can see the piles of the original Virginia and Tennessee Railroad Bridge. (Stop #5)

Stop #5 – The Destruction of the New River Railroad Bridge – May 10, 1864

On the evening of May 9, 1864, McCausland's defeated army fell back to the vital railroad bridge over the New River. The west approach to the bridge was protected by a strong fort with an in-place battery. Fearful that he could not hold the fort and that his troops would be trapped by the river, McCausland decided to try to defend the bridge from the other side, the east bank, using artillery fire. He took the six guns from the fort, spiking two that were too big to carry off. Taking all the ammunition his tired men could carry, he crossed the river using several barges. On the other side, his men were so tired that they collapsed without digging emplacements for the guns.

At 4:00 a.m. May 10, Crook had his men up, and at work ravishing the supply center of Dublin Depot. While some were taking bacon and ammunition, others were preparing to blow up what they couldn't carry. Just after first light, the army began to move east toward the vital Bridge. One rear guard unit barely got clear of town before the fires set off a great explosion. One Yank wrote, "Bursting shells created a noise and confusion that could have been amusing had it not been so dangerous."

As they marched, squads of men tore up the rail tracks, using fire to heat and twist the iron rails. Every culvert and small bridge was destroyed along the six-mile stretch to the river.

Just before 9:00 a.m. the lead Union forces approached the bridge. Central Depot, on the other side of the river, had been a small town of only 20 homes before the war. The war had made it the focal point of four years of attempts by the Union armies to destroy the bridge. Now they were there.

McCausland's 14 guns under the command of Captain Thomas Bryan tried to keep the Yanks away. By 10:00 a.m. Crook had brought up the 12 guns of Glassie and McMullen, beginning a two-hour artillery duel, at the relatively close range of 800-1000 yards. One early shot forced Crook to dismount. The Confederates, thinking he was hit, gave a great cheer.

There were acts of bravery. A shell with a burning fuse landed under one of the Union guns. Pvt. John Wilhoff grabbed the shell, cut off the fuse, and tossed it aside. If it had exploded, it could have wiped out the entire section.

The Union guns had the real advantage.

Sgt. Milton Humphreys described it, *"The Federal position was superior for two reasons, one of which was the fact that it was more elevated, and the other, that it could be seen where every shot struck, whereas from the Confederate position it was not possible to see where a projectile struck unless it went too low. The difficulty of hitting a target on the horizon or sky-line is notorious."*

Humphreys was right. The Confederates fired more than 750 rounds without hitting a single Union gun. The Union fire wasn't much better. Only a few were killed or wounded. There was one unusual death. When Lt. Col. Hayes brought his troops to the river, he ordered them to get down and take cover. All of them did except for a dismounted trooper from the 5th W. Va. Cavalry who looked up and said to Hayes, "Why don't you get off your horse, too?" Hayes continued to order the trooper to take cover. The stubborn reply was, "I'll get down when you do." A shell exploded killing the Private.

When they examined the body, they discovered it was a woman. There is tantalizingly little evidence as to the identity of the woman. One story was that her father and brother had been killed by Confederate neighbors, and seeking revenge, she had joined the army. Recent studies have shown that a surprising number of women fought in the war disguised as men.

As the ineffective two-hour bombardment began to exhaust ammunition on both sides, Crook sent several units of sharpshooters to the riverside, giving cover to those sent to set fire to the bridge. Capt. Michael Egan, 15th W. Va., was able to crawl out and set fire to the dry pine siding. Several rail cars loaded with combustibles were pushed onto the bridge. Soon the 780' long, 56' high covered bridge was in flames. Firing on both sides stopped as all were transfixed by the conflagration. The band of the 23rd Ohio began to play "Yankee Doodle."

Capt. Wilson, 12th Ohio, wrote, *"Clouds of heavy black smoke rolled out of the ends and poured through every crevice and crack, like a boiler under heavy pressure of steam, until suddenly the flames burst through, and the bridge seemed to leap into the air from its piers, and plunge, a mass of ruins into the river below."*

When the smoke cleared, the wooden structure and tracks were gone, but the metal outer structure and piers of the 8-year-old bridge were still there. Crook had neglected to bring explosives that could blow the remains. He tried to use solid shot from his guns; the balls just bounced off. Yet the bridge, as a usable entity, was gone.

With mission accomplished, Crook quickly turned north, and marched downstream for Peppers Ferry and a passage to the other side of the river. The Confederates rapidly fell back to Christiansburg. Without adequate transportation, Crook had to leave his wounded behind, hoping for good care by the local Confederates. As he approached the New River, his column was significantly enlarged by over a thousand blacks who wanted to escape to freedom. By evening the rain began to fall.

more than 4,500 men and artillery at Saltville, making that an impossible target for his weak column.

Near Tazewell, a Yank soldier killed in a skirmish was buried in the garden of C. H. Greever. A few days later, a neighbor asked Greever if he was sorry to have a Yank buried so near his home. Greever replied, "No, ding it, I wish they were all in there."

In the dark of night on May 8, and as quietly as possible, Averell changed his course, headed toward Princeton, and went over East River Mountain into Rocky Gap. He was now a day behind Crook. On May 9 he turned south on the Turnpike heading for Wytheville, and a chance to strike the railroad or lead mines. He was not aware that on the same day Crook was fighting at Cloyd's Mountain. Along the way snipers harassed the Union column. Averell ordered his men to grab civilians as hostages, interspersing them among his men. Effective security, but slowing down his march. He also seized a small, but much needed, Confederate wagon train of food supplies. His troops would have a few more days of food.

The Confederates responded to Averell's threat. General W. E. "Grumble" Jones had a small brigade of cavalry to protect Tazewell and Saltville, and General John Morgan had another cavalry brigade at Abingdon. They rushed to block the raiders. The 19th Va. Cavalry was sent to Wytheville. Morgan's Kentucky Cavalry chased through Tazewell, but instead of following the Union raiders to Rocky Gap, they went up through Burkes Garden, a short cut to Wytheville, arriving there the night of May 9.

Morgan took charge of both the arriving regulars and local militia. He decided to defend Wytheville two miles north of town, on the Raleigh-Grayson Turnpike, where it passed through the narrow gap between Queen's Knob and Cove Mountain. By midday May 10, Confederates had set up a barricade of fallen trees and had the 16th Va. Cavalry, and elements of the 8th Va. Cavalry with one gun blocking the road. The rest of Morgan and Jones' men were coming quickly. The Confederates would have slightly fewer troops than the Union on the battlefield, but closely matched.

By 4:00 p.m. Averell was at the Gap, and decided to try to push through the Confederates. (See Map 38.) The 14th Pa. was sent up the mountain for a flank attack on the left of the 16th Va. On the right, the 34th Ohio dismounted and attacked the 8th Va. barricade, while the 2nd W. Va. Cavalry prepared a straight-on cavalry charge down the road. Col. William Graham shouted for his 16th Va. Cavalry to "dismount boys and follow Grimes," a unique military order which had always meant "Go for them, boys."

The attack by the 14th Pa. was stopped. By 5:00 p.m. the Union advance ended. Morgan's Cavalry arrived, going around the mountain to hit the Union left. Averell was hit. Lt. James Abraham noted, *"A musket ball cut the scalp across his forehead. He bled profusely. Binding a handkerchief over the wound, he kept his saddle."* The Yanks fell back to Millers Ridge and went over to the defensive.

There was a hard fight. Lt. Abraham described the next two hours: *"We repulsed a second and third charge in the*

THE CIVIL WAR IN THE NEW RIVER VALLEY

Map 38

Cove Mountain Battle
May 10, 1864

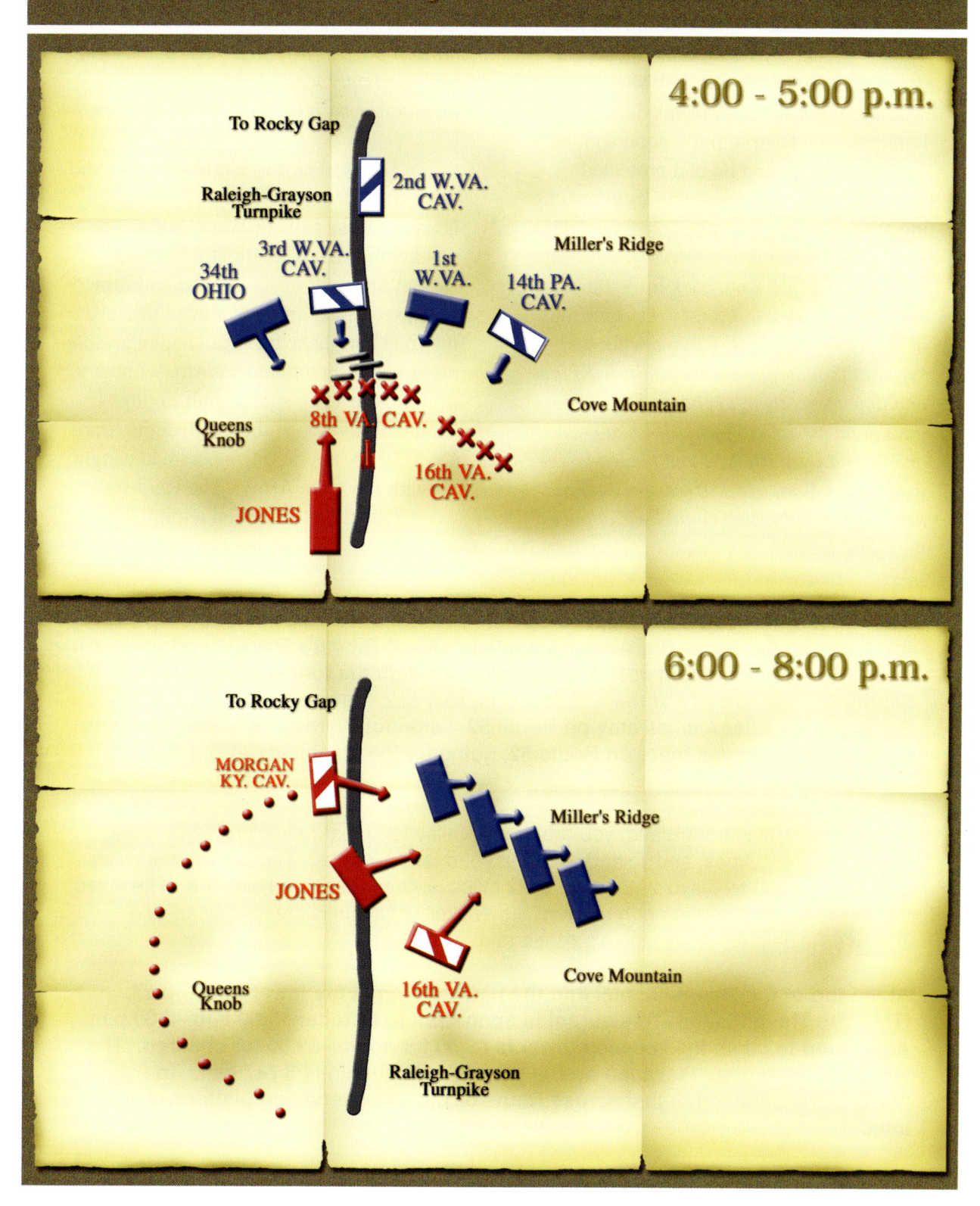

4:00 - 5:00 p.m.

To Rocky Gap
Raleigh-Grayson Turnpike
2nd W.VA. CAV.
3rd W.VA. CAV.
34th OHIO
1st W.VA.
14th PA. CAV.
Miller's Ridge
Queens Knob
8th VA. CAV.
16th VA. CAV.
Cove Mountain
JONES

6:00 - 8:00 p.m.

To Rocky Gap
MORGAN KY. CAV.
JONES
Miller's Ridge
Queens Knob
16th VA. CAV.
Cove Mountain
Raleigh-Grayson Turnpike

dusk of the evening. We, when night closed around us withdrew – having as one of the boys expressed it, 'sawed off more than we could bring away.'"

Averell was beaten, and now moved up Walker Creek, crossed the mountain and was in Dublin by nightfall of May 11, sending word to Crook of his difficulties. Later, Averell tried to put a good spin on his loss by claiming he had protected Crook by preventing Morgan from attacking at Cloyd's Mountain!

The Confederates went back to Wytheville, tired but victorious. Morgan was generous in describing the victory to his wife: *"Averell fought his men elegantly, tried time and time to get them to charge but our boys gave them no time to form. If I had been one hour later this place and the lead mines would have been lost....If we had 2 more hours of daylight [we] could have captured the entire force."*

The Union force had lost 114 killed and wounded; the Confederates lost about 40. Averell had to leave his wounded for Confederate care.

Lt. Abraham lamented, *"This is one of the hardest parts of raiding, you cannot bring off your badly wounded but must leave them to the mercies of an infuriated foe."*

Averell pushed east to Christiansburg, did more damage to the rail tracks, but then headed for the hills of West Virginia, a day behind Crook's retreating column. He ran into McCausland, who had turned to chase Crook, and was forced to leave the road and make an almost unbelievable night march in a thunderstorm, without a trail, up the steep side of Salt Pond Mountain to escape the Confederate trap. On May 15, his tired troopers had caught up with the main Army. The Raid was over. One target had been temporarily destroyed.

After driving through Cove Gap, "Stop #6," you will drive 18.3 miles to Stop #7, the tower on the top of Big Walker Mountain, site of Toland's Raid. Continue north on I-77 for 9 miles to Exit #52. You will pass through the tunnel under Big Walker Mountain. Turn off I-77 at the exit of Bland, Exit #52. Turn left going south on Route 52-42. After 4 miles stay on Route 52 – sign for Wytheville. Route 42 turns right. Drive 3.3 miles more on Route 52, going up the steep side of Big Walker Mountain.

As you drive south from Bland, you are on the valley road that runs along Big Walker Creek. Averell, Crook, and Toland used this road for their raids. The pass through Big Walker Mountain to Cloyd's Mountain is 22 miles north of Bland on Route 42. The steep road – Route 52 – up the north slope of Big Walker Mountain is the road used by Toland's Raiders for an escape after their raid.

At the top of the Mountain, pull into the parking area at the tower for Stop #7. (TM-139) The gift shop – restaurant is open April to October 10:00 a.m.–6:00 p.m. Admission to climb the 200-step tower is $3.50 for adults–$2.50 for children. The view is spectacular. Elevation on the top of the Mountain is 3,787 feet. To the north of the parking lot, just across Route 621 is an observation platform–a free look.

THE CIVIL WAR IN THE NEW RIVER VALLEY

Panoramic view from Big Walker Mountain looking north

Looking north, on the immediate left is Garden Mountain (Burkes Garden); in front is Round Mountain. In the distance you can see East River Mountain that forms the boundary between Virginia and West Virginia. Bluefield and Princeton are out of sight just north of East River Mountain. Route 621 coming up the mountain from the left is the route used by Toland as he crossed from Burkes Garden. From the Tower, or back windows of the Gift Shop, you can look south toward Wytheville 12 miles away.

Panoramic view from Big Walker Mountain looking south

Stop #7– Toland's Raid – July 13–23, 1863
Approach and Escape

We go back a year, to the summer of 1863. In the first week of July, Lee's invasion of Pennsylvania resulted in the Battle of Gettysburg and withdrawal back to Virginia. In the same week, Grant captured Vicksburg in Mississippi. Then the Union commanders wanted to renew the offensive in the New River theater.

After Cox's failure in 1862, they were still trying to find the right composition for a successful raiding force. (See Day Two Tour.) In July, they launched a small mobile force on the west side of the New

Toland's Route
July 17 - 21, 1863

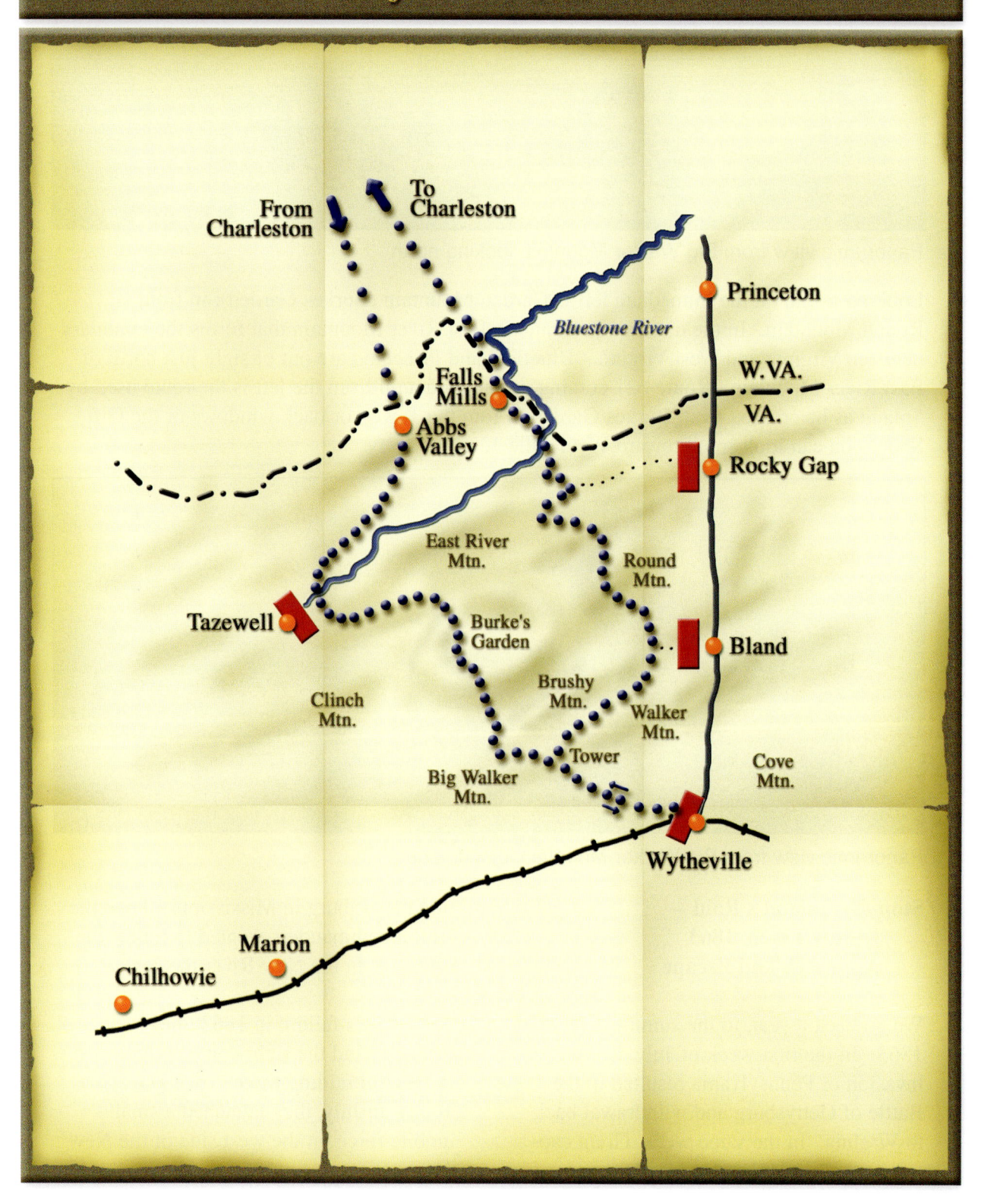

THE CIVIL WAR IN THE NEW RIVER VALLEY

River, hoping to strike at one or more of the strategic targets, to do damage, and then to escape before the Confederates could effectively react.

Nine hundred men were assembled, led by Col. John Toland consisting of his 34th Ohio Infantry, which had just become a mounted unit in May 1863; Col. William Powell's 2nd W. Va. Cavalry, and Captain Denis Delaney with two companies of the 1st W. Va. Cavalry; a light force with no artillery or wagon train. None of the leaders would return: Toland and Delaney were killed, and Powell was wounded and captured.

Wanting to circle around McCausland's Brigade, which was on the Raleigh-Grayson Turnpike between Beckley and Flat Top, Toland on July 13 moved from Charleston toward Logan and Wyoming counties (the route that Averell would use in 1864). Early on July 17 they emerged from the mountains, making first contact by gobbling up a detachment of Confederate pickets in Abbs Valley just north of Tazewell. One got away and quickly spread the word of the raid.

The Confederates from the beginning were confused about where the raiders might be going, but alerted their leaders, who tried to assemble forces to stop and trap the raiders. After spending the day burning a flour mill, Toland camped just east of Jeffersonville (Tazewell) near the home of Samuel Tynes. During the night, Tynes learned that the objective was Wytheville, and in the early hours he sent his 26-year-old daughter Mary on horseback to sound the alarm to Wytheville, 45 miles and four mountains away.

Before dawn, July 18, the raiders bypassed Jeffersonville, moved around East River Mountain, turned right, and went up through Burkes Garden. Col. Andrew Mays, with 125 troopers of the newly organized 10th Ky. Cavalry, caught up to the rearguard going up the mountain, released the Confederates caught the day before, and captured Capt. Cutter and 15 men of the 34th Ohio. The small column would be in trouble if the Confederates acted together and quickly. In the early afternoon, Toland crossed Big Walker Mountain (Stop #7), and moved to Wytheville just 12 miles away to attack the railroad and bridges that he could get to.

(We will look at the Battle of Wytheville at Stop #8.)

After the battle, at 10:00 p.m. that same night, July 18, the raiding column, now led by Col. Freeman Franklin (Toland had been killed), left Wytheville with nearly 100 captives and returned to the top of Big Walker Mountain. The day had been long, the Union troops having ridden more than 60 miles up and down mountains and having fought a battle. You can see how difficult the terrain is and can only imagine how tired they were, but with thousands of Confederates trying to capture them, they were motivated to move fast.

The next morning, July 19, they lightened their load by releasing the prisoners. Changing their route, they went down Big Walker Mountain over the "Ram's Head"–the way you came up on Route 52. McCausland had moved south from Princeton through Rocky Gap, and had forward elements as far as Bland. The Raleigh-Grayson Turnpike way out was blocked. General Williams sent more cavalry from Saltville and had the roads from Tazewell blocked.

The raiders left the road, and went over Round Mountain, without even a trail. They found both ends of the valley before East River Mountain blocked, so again left the road, went up a narrow trail and crossed over the mountain followed by a detachment of frustrated Confederate cavalry in pursuit. Coming down East River Mountain, the raiders pushed on to Falls Mills, where they rounded up some cattle and camped for the night.

Early the next morning, July 20, they were up before dawn and headed for the high mountains of West Virginia. The Confederates arrived too late and only hit a rearguard force. The Yanks had gotten away, arriving back at Charleston on July 23.

Aftermath–
The Confederates had stopped the raid without major damage. They had five times as many men in the area as there were raiders, but failed to trap them. A war of words began, with each commander blaming someone else for the failure to catch the raiders. There were serious command problems. The Yanks learned that the strategic targets were vulnerable, but a small raiding force was too light to destroy the objectives. They would need both more power and more deception for success. These were lessons to build on for Averell's Raids, August–December 1863. (See Day Two Tour.)

"Mr. Yank . . . was completely cowed . . . ."

Pvt. James Sedinger, 8th Va. Cavalry, wrote of a poignant incident as the Yanks fled Virginia. A Union soldier of the 34th Ohio, who went to a house where only a girl was at home, and demanded food and a horse. While he was distracted, the girl grabbed his rifle, *"....found that it was loaded, then presented to Mr. Yank and told him to throw up his hands or she would shoot."* She took him prisoner, and when Sedinger arrived, *"Mr. Yank looked to me as if he thought he ought to be hung. He was completely cowed by his experience with a mountain girl of Virginia."* Raiding was not always easy.

> **Leaving the parking lot at the Tower, you will drive 13 miles to Wytheville. Turn right from the parking area continuing south on Route 52. After 12 miles you will go under I-81. Stay on Route 21 – North 4th Street – into town. At the second light, turn left on Monroe Street. Go one block on Monroe Street and turn left on Tazewell Street. Park on the right side of the street in the parking area across from the Rock House Museum. (Stop #8.) (TM-153)**
>
> You may visit the Rock House Museum, which is open June–October during the middle of the day. Admission, $2.00 for adults, $.75 for children.

Stop #8 – The Battle of Wytheville–
–July 18, 1863 –
Toland's Raid

By mid-afternoon on July 18, Toland's columns had penetrated the Confederate line of defense that stretched from Tazewell, through Princeton, to The Narrows.

He was approaching the supply and railroad town of Wytheville, not expecting much opposition. Just before entering town he dispatched two squadrons south to cut the telegraph and to destroy the rails and depot at Mount Airey (now Rural Retreat). Without a reliable local guide, he did not dare send other squads to the north. As the raiders entered town a little after 5:00 p.m., they found the town was not undefended.

The Confederates had been warned by Mary Tynes. District Commander General Sam Jones, at Dublin, was using the telegraph and railroad to rush any available force to Wytheville. At Dublin, a passenger train was stopped, civilians unloaded, and by 3:00 p.m. two companies of infantry under Major Thomas Bowyer, and two guns of Capt. John Oliver, a force of 130, were sent down the line. They unloaded at the depot south of town at 5:10 p.m., as the Yanks entered from the north.

In town, Col. Abraham Umberger and Major Joseph Kent were organizing the local militia, townsmen and transient soldiers who numbered about 120 old men and boys. Rifles were distributed from the supply depot. The rag-tag force was placed in the buildings along the streets that they expected the raiders to use, forming a house to house defense. Altogether the defenders would have a force of nearly 250, but would be badly outnumbered and outgunned.

With enemy forces arriving by train and cavalry in pursuit from behind, Toland decided not to take time to deploy and attack the town from the flanks. Instead he ordered a charge right down the streets. The battle was on.

Capt. Delaney, 1st W. Va. Cavalry, and Col. William Powell, 2nd W. Va. Cavalry, lined up, drew sabers, and charged in columns of four down the streets. The fire from the houses killed Delaney. Major Hoffman, 2nd Cavalry, reported, *"Colonel Powell was severely wounded in the back by a revolver fired by one of our men, and left the field. My horse was shot and I was thrown over his head...."*

In the first ten minutes, near the top of the hill Col. Toland was hit and killed. Col. Franklin took command, stopped the use-

THE CIVIL WAR IN THE NEW RIVER VALLEY

Map 40: Toland's Raid at Wytheville
July 18, 1863

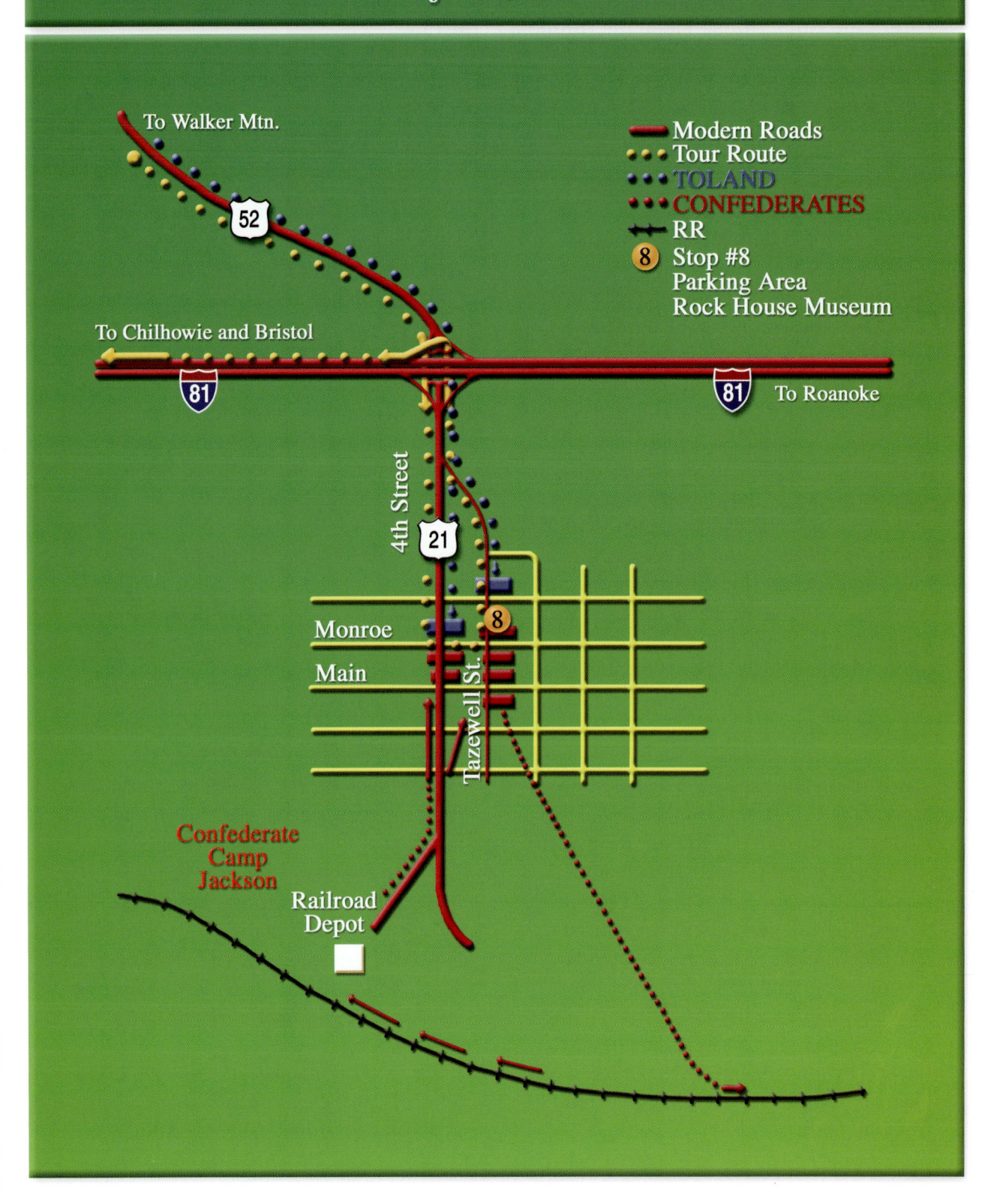

Legend:
- Modern Roads
- Tour Route
- TOLAND
- CONFEDERATES
- RR
- ⑧ Stop #8 Parking Area Rock House Museum

Map labels:
- To Walker Mtn.
- 52
- To Chilhowie and Bristol
- 81
- 81 To Roanoke
- 4th Street
- 21
- Monroe
- Main
- Tazewell St.
- Confederate Camp Jackson
- Railroad Depot

less cavalry charges, dismounted the 34th Ohio and began a vicious house-to-house attack. Jones later reported, *"One of their wounded men, who had crawled into one of those houses is believed to have been burned. His screams were heard and his charred bones found in the ruins …. A Roman Catholic priest, while endeavoring to rescue a decrepit woman from a burning house, was shot and so severely wounded that his leg had to be amputated."*

Captain Oliver was captured and reportedly killed. Col. Franklin wrote in his official report, *"The contest, of most obstinate hand-to-hand fighting, lasted about one and one-half hours. We, however, carried the town by storm and with a perfect rush. The principle among the rebels seemed to be 'no quarter' and we took them on their own principle for a time, until they were entirely subdued, and as the soldier, citizens, and even women fired from their houses, both public and private, we burned the town to ashes."*

Major Bowyer's men fell back to the railroad, but found their train had backed away. They headed for Dublin on foot, up the tracks. One of Oliver's guns was captured, hauled away, and eventually discarded in the Union retreat the next day. Nearly 100 soldiers and townsmen were captured and later released on Big Walker Mountain. The raiders lost 15 killed and 40 some wounded or missing. The Confederates had less than 10 killed and an undetermined number wounded. The shooting was over by 8:00 p.m.; and for the next two hours the raiders fired the depot, tore up some track, and burned much of the town.

At 10:00 p.m. Franklin, fearful of Confederates coming by train, decided to retreat. (Commentary is back at Stop #7.) The battle was a defeat for the local defenders, but only minimal damage was done to the railroad, and none to the lead mines south of town. Wytheville would be the target of attacks again in 1864 and 1865.

A note on Colonel William Powell, 2nd W. Va. Cavalry. We met him on the Day Two Tour as a "spy," then a raider, even a house burner. He was known and hated by the Confederates. His wound was not serious, but he was captured. He was not treated as a "regular" prisoner of war. General Jones insisted that Powell was a war criminal, had him shipped in chains to Libby prison in Richmond, where he was put in solitary confinement on bread and water. He was forced to stand trial. After being acquitted of killing prisoners but found guilty of unlawful destruction of property, he was exchanged, promoted to Brigadier General, and was back to fighting with his 2nd Cavalry at Cove Gap in May 1864. In 1865 he was assigned to catch "Bushwhackers" in the lower Shenandoah Valley, where he was not so generous with his captives, having several of them executed. After the war he returned to his iron business and politics back in West Virginia. In 1893 he was awarded the Congressional Medal of Honor for the Sinking Creek Raid in 1862.

> **Leaving the parking area, you will drive 44 miles to Stop #9 – Saltville.**
> **Turn right and continue up the hill on Tazewell Street.** At the top of the hill you are near the spot where Col. Toland was killed. **Go 1 mile on Tazewell Street until the road ends at a Stop sign. You are back on 4th Street. You can see the Interstate (I-81) to your right. Turn right, get to the left lane, and turn left onto I-81 going south toward Bristol. You will be on I-81 for 36 miles.**
>
> Near mile marker 39, you will go by Seven Mile Ford. Notice both the river and the tracks of the railroad going from Wytheville toward Bristol. In December 1864 near the Ford, General Breckenridge was defeated by General Stoneman leaving Saltville open to attack. (See Stop #11.)
>
> **Leave I-81 at Exit 35 – Chilhowie – Route 107. Turn right on Route 107 toward Saltville.** At 3.8 miles, you will be going through Lyon's Gap, crossing Big Walker Mountain, the first barrier of mountains that shielded Saltville. **Go just over seven miles on Route 107 to the "Scenic Overlook," going down the hill, just before Saltville. Go slowly. The Overlook is on the left just past a bend in the road. Turn left into the Overlook for Stop #9. (TM-197)**

The view approaching Saltville

Stop #9 – Saltville Overlook –
The Saltville Campaigns
–October – December 1864–

The salt works at Saltville were one of the three strategic targets that Union commanders had been trying to destroy since the opening months of the War in 1861. Tucked away in a beautiful natural mountain fortress, Saltville was the most inaccessible of the Union goals, and would not come under direct attack until the fall of 1864. From the Overlook, you can see the town and ponds that were once the brine wells for the salt industry. Salt began to be mined here as early as the 1790s. The salt was 200' down in a 200' thick strata, deep mined at first, and then pumped to the surface, boiled and evaporated to form the salt crystals.

Nineteenth century America was much more dependent on salt than we today. Salt was needed to cure beef and pork, the staples of diet, as well as to cure leather, which a horse-drawn society was dependent upon. The business prospered in the 1850s with the arrival of a spur line of the Virginia and Tennessee Railroad in 1856.

In 1861, the main company was under the leadership of William Stuart, the older brother of the soon to be famous cavalry leader, J. E. B. Stuart. Only five commercially useable sources of salt were in the South at the outset of the War. Three of them quickly fell into Union hands: Kanawha Salines in West Virginia, the Kentucky mines, and the Louisiana mines. The works in Alabama and at Saltville became essential for the Confederacy. At Saltville, even with a rapidly expanded operation, the boiling pots could not keep up with demand. By 1863 they were producing more than 3,000 bushels a day.

The shortage of labor was as crucial as security.

Raids on Saltville began in 1862 and came from three directions. The first approach, as we have already seen, was from the New River Valley of West Virginia – Toland's Raid in 1863 and Averell's in May 1864.

A second approach was through the rough mountain gaps between Virginia and Kentucky. General Samuel Carter, with 1,000 Union Cavalry, tried that way, unsuccessfully, in 1862. We will look at General Stephen Burbridge's attempt in October 1864 at **Stops #10a, 10b, and 10c** of this tour.

The third approach was through the mountain gaps from Tennessee and then up the valley through Bristol and Abingdon. Using the southern approach, in December of 1864 General George Stoneman succeeded in destroying the wells – Stop #11.

Before leaving the Overlook to examine the Battles for Saltville, notice the surrounding terrain. (See Map 41.) You approach Saltville from the south, roughly along the route used in 1864 by Stoneman. From the front of the Overlook, looking north over the town, in the distance you see the high mountain, Flat Top. Behind that, out of sight, there are two more mountains, Clinch and Paint Lick, before the Clinch River Valley, and then the mountains that border on Kentucky. The smaller mountain in front of you is Little Mountain.

There are five gaps or passes through Little Mountain: Hayter Gap–10 miles south, Allison Gap–just behind the right

Saltville Area

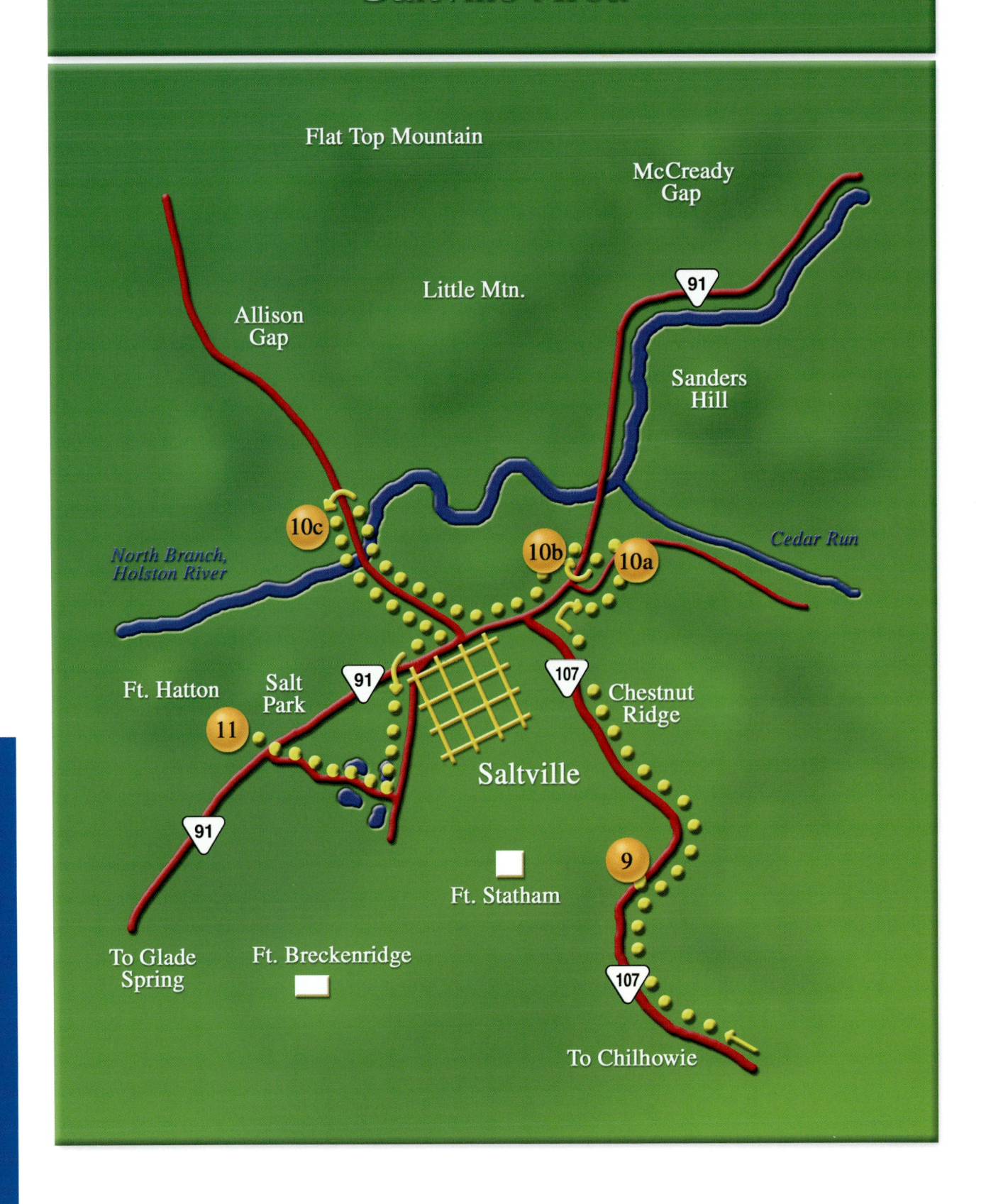

Map 41

side of town, McCready Gap, Laurel Creek, and Low Gap, the last three being off in the distance to the far right.

The Confederates would never have enough troops to effectively block all the gaps and would have to establish a defense line closer to town. Burbridge's Raid came from the North through Low Gap and Allison Gap (Stop #10c). Turn left, behind the Overlook. The high ground on the left is where Fort Statham was, with Fort Breckenridge further behind. To the front left, across the road was Fort Hatton.

These three forts, which guarded against an attack from the south, played no role in Burbridge's October attack and were overrun in Stoneman's December attack. (After completing the Tour in Saltville, if you choose to exit along "Burbridge's Advance," you will be following the troop's route across Flat Top and Clinch Mountain through Tazewell.)

In the fall of 1864, General William Sherman had captured Atlanta and was on his way into Georgia on his "March to the Sea." In Tennessee, Thomas was meeting the threat of Hood. In central Virginia, Grant had fought at Cold Harbor and was laying siege to Petersburg and Richmond. In the lower Shenandoah Valley, General Phil Sheridan with Crook and Averell was facing General Jubal Early's Confederates, including many of the seasoned New River veterans of Breckenridge such as the 22nd Va., 36th Va., 8th Va. Cavalry. The upper New River Valley was largely stripped of troops.
In eastern Kentucky in mid-September, General Stephen Burbridge planned a raid on Saltville. He wanted a force much like Crook's that had hit the New River Bridge in May. With some 4,500 cavalry, mounted infantry, and a battery of mountain howitzers, he would go through the mountains to hit Saltville from the north, while a force of 2,000 cavalry would threaten the Tennessee gaps as had Averell's flank column in May.

Burbridge's career was at its height. He was a 32-year-old Kentucky plantation slave owner who had chosen to stay loyal to the Union. As a lawyer, he had only minimal military training, but he started the war in 1861 as the Colonel of the loyal 26th Ky. Infantry. He had risen to command a Department in East Kentucky after his successful capture of the confederate raider, John Morgan. Throughout the war, Burbridge had treated Confederate Kentuckians harshly, earning a hated reputation that was heightened when he advocated creating military combat units of black soldiers. He had begun creating those units, including the 5th and 6th U.S. Colored Cavalry.

On September 26th, 1864, Burbridge's column began to move through the rugged east Kentucky mountains, even as he learned that he would not get the flanking column because those troops were needed in Tennessee. He would do it alone, with a much lighter force than Crook had in May, but now the Confederates also had less strength.

The Confederates only had a token force at Saltville. When they learned of the approaching Union column, they began to send all available men toward Saltville. Small units were sent to Clinch Mountain to block the passes and buy time. The race was on. By Oct. 1 Burbridge with 4,500 was over Clinch and Flat Top holding the vital bridge and middle of the line.

The 250 men of the 13th Va. Reserve Battalion, local white-shirted militia led by Lt. Col. Robert Smith, were poorly placed out front on Sanders Hill and refused to come back to Chestnut Ridge. The 350 militia of Lt. Col. Robert Preston's 4th Va. Reserve, some from as far away as Wytheville, were placed in entrenchments closer to town. They were not expected to do much.

At almost the last minute, the 1,400 Confederates from the Army of the Tennessee that had been 10 miles south at Hayter's Gap arrived, under the command of General John Williams, who was no stranger to the area, having been in command here on 1862-1863. Williams sent Col. George Dibrell's 4th, 8th, 13th Tennessee Cavalry to the rifle pits on the right of Chestnut Ridge and put young Gen. Felix Robertson's Confederate Cavalry units to the center of Chestnut Ridge. His third unit, Col. William Breckenridge's 9th Ky. Cavalry, was on the far left guarding the Allison Gap bridge.

The fighting began about 10:00 a.m. and lasted for nearly six hours. Starting from the Confederate right on Sanders Hill and moving to the left, Ratliff's Brigade with his black troops on the left flank first hit the militia on Sanders Hill. All of the Union Brigade had either Spencer Repeating or other breech-loading rifles, both out-gunning and out-numbering the militia. Possibly motivated by hatred for Negroes fighting, the Confederate militia fought with determination, only slowly being pushed across Cedar Creek and up Chestnut Ridge.

The black soldiers and the rest of Ratliff's

Chestnut Ridge

Overlooking the Holston River bridge

Brigade pushed to Dibrell and Robertson's line and engaged in close, vicious fighting. One Confederate officer was so enraged by the sight of black soldiers that he charged into them firing a pistol and was immediately killed. Artillery fire from the top of the Ridge pounded the attackers. After several hours, as ammunition ran out, the Union Brigade fell back. Seventy percent of the Union casualties that day came in the fight on Chestnut Ridge. Both white and black fought with courage.

The next morning, after the Union force had retreated, an incident scarred the valor of the fight, "the Saltville Massacre."

Armed Confederates entered a field hospital on Sanders Hill, dragged wounded black soldiers out, and killed them! There has been a long controversy over the number killed. Claims range from nearly 100 to 5. Recent studies put the number at about 10 there on Sanders Hill, as well as later at another location. Even ten prisoners murdered, because of race hatred, was an atrocity denounced then and now.

No one was ever tried for these murders.

With the Yanks unable to take Chestnut Ridge, the fighting shifted to the cemetery on Elizabeth Hill. **(Stop #10b.)**

Leaving Stop #10a, drive 0.5 mile to Stop #10c, Elizabeth Cemetery. Turn right on Buckeye Street and return the way you came from Route 91. At Route 91 turn right. Go about 0.1 mile and turn left into the Cemetery. Go to the left of the silver cannon and turn right onto the one-lane road through the Cemetery. On the right you will pass the markers for the Stuart family sites. At the end loop of the Cemetery there is a place for several vehicles to park on the right side of the road. (Stop #10b).

You may want to walk out to the steep sides of the hill looking over the Holston River below. In 1864, the Cemetery covered only a small portion of the hill near the main road.

Stop #10b –First Battle of Saltville – Elizabeth Hill Cemetery –Assault on the Center–

By noon Oct. 2, 1864, Col. Hobson had crossed the flat ground of Broddy's Bottom, dismounted his infantry and sent them across the river and up the steep vegetation-covered hill.

Col. Edwin Trimble's 10th Ky. Cavalry was outnumbered and fell back toward the Cemetery. Trimble had begun the war as a private in Floyd's army in 1861 at Kessler's Cross Lanes; now he led a battalion. Brigade commander, Col. Giltner, sent some of the men from his left to help and went looking for more. He had no authority over the militia reserve, Preston's 4th Va., but called them forward from their safe trenches in the rear. Armed with Belgian rifles, the militia had boasted they were going to "shoot a nigger." Now they were called forward to face the white Kentucky riflemen. The militia fired one weak volley, and turned and ran back to their entrenchments with only a few casualties. With sword waving and shouting, Col. Trimble rallied his men, and with help from the 10th Va. Mounted Infantry charged the Yanks. The tired and surprised Yanks retreated from the hill. Col. Trimble and four other officers lay dead, but the center had held, as the fighting shifted to the left flank. **(Stop #10c.)**

Leaving the Cemetery drive 1.2 miles to Stop #10c on Allison Gap Road. Turn right on Route 91, south toward Saltville. Drive 0.6 mile until the traffic light. Turn right. Drive 0.6 mile on Allison Gap Road. Go slowly as you cross the Holston River on the Elizabeth Norris Bridge. Thirty yards past the bridge, turn left into the small parking area bordered by chain link fences. (Stop #10c.)

You can look back at the position of the Confederates on the mountain, on the other side of the river, guarding the pass you just drove through. The attacking Yanks would not get much closer than where you are now.

Mountain panorama outside Saltville

Pulloff area with American flag

Stop #10c – The First Battle of Saltville – Allison Gap – October 2, 1864

General Charles Hanson's brigade, the largest in the force, spent several hours trying to work their way around the Confederate left, squeezing along the river and the slope of Middle Mountain. A road from Allison Gap crossed the Holston River and then went through a narrow pass into the town. Confederates from Col. William Breckenridge's (cousin of General Breckenridge) 9th Ky. Cavalry and the left flank of Giltner's 4th Ky. Cavalry held the high ground on both sides of the pass, shooting at the Yanks as they moved along the other side of the river.

The Yanks never had a chance against this mountain bastion, losing more than 40 men just trying to get into position. For the Confederates on the heights it was an easy day.

George Mosgrove, 4th Ky. Cavalry, described the Confederate experience.

"They would fire a volley and then yell, 'Come right up and draw your salt!' Silas Simms, a dead-shot, would draw a bead on a blue-coat, blaze away and then hail the 'Yank' with the interrogatory, 'How's that; am I shooting too high or too low?' Afterwards, while passing over the field, Simms came upon the body of a dead officer whose head had been partially torn away by a cannon ball. The unsympathetic Confederate with grim humor, took a handful of salt from his haversack and threw it into the cavity in the dead officer's head, saying, 'There, you came for salt, now take some.'"

The Union brigade fell back, Hanson wounded, severely "gutshot." By 5:00 p.m. as the firing died down, a great cheer spread along the Confederate line. Generals Breckenridge and Echols had arrived. Burbridge now had fears of a "phantom" Confederate force arriving. During the evening the Yanks built large fires hoping that the Confederates would think they were getting ready for another assault in the morning. In the dark of night, Burbridge ordered a retreat.

He turned over command to Col. Hanson and then with haste rode away back to Kentucky. Hanson was forced to leave his wounded and moved the force quickly back the way they had come. There was a weak pursuit back as far as Tazewell, but the Confederates were just glad to see the raiders gone with no damage to the salt works.

The Yanks had lost more than 100 killed and 150 wounded captured. Confederate losses are difficult to determine, probably 30-50 killed and 100 wounded. Several captured soldiers were released during the Union retreat. The first Battle for Saltville was over, the salt works had been saved, but in only two months the town would be attacked again. **(Stop #11.)**

Leaving Stop #10c drive 2 miles to Stop #11, Salt Park. Turn right on Allison Gap Road and go 0.6 mile back through the pass into Saltville. Turn right at the light on Route 91. Go only 50 yards. Leave Route 91 and bear left. The sign points to Museum of Middle Appalachians. Go 0.5 mile on Palmer Drive. Just after you pass the first Salt Pond, turn right on the road through Wellfields Recreation Park.

You may want to stop at any of the pull-outs to enjoy the scenery. There is a picnic shelter on the left. **Drive to the end of the road. Turn left on Route 91, West Main Street. Go 50 yards and turn right into the Salt Park.**

At Salt Park...

Salt Park contains reconstructions of the equipment used to produce salt. There are picnic benches. **(Stop #11.)**

Pictured at left: the pavilion at Salt Park housing a salt furnace.

Below: A "walking beam" pump.

Stop #11 – The Second Battle of Saltville – Stoneman's Raids – Dec. 20, 1864–March 1865

After the October battle, General Williams' troops were sent to Georgia to face Sherman. Most of General Breckenridge's force was sent to the lower Shenandoah and to Richmond, leaving only a handful to guard the salt wells and lead mines. In November, General George Stoneman began to plan another raid.

Stoneman had spent most of the war leading cavalry raids in both the East and West. In the summer of 1864 he had been captured in an unsuccessful raid to free Union prisoners at Andersonville, Ga. After having been exchanged, he wanted to redeem himself. As commander of the Dept. of Ohio, he organized a force of 5,500.

General Burbridge, with his Division of 4,000 from the mountains of Kentucky, would join Col. Alvin Gillem's brigade of cavalry of 1,500 and move from Bristol and Abingdon into Southwest Virginia. On Dec. 15, the raiders easily pushed aside a force of 600 and moved up the road toward Chilhowie. In Saltville, Breckenridge assembled a force of 1,400 to meet the threat.

On Dec. 15, Stoneman made the choice not to move on Saltville, but continue up the valley toward Wytheville with its lead mines and the newly rebuilt New River Bridge. At Wytheville on Dec. 16, the town was ravished once again by two regiments that went south to the lead mines and destroyed much of the works and equipment. A smaller force went all the way to Central Depot and tried to burn the new bridge that had been built over the New River, but the green timbers would not be set on fire. Dec. 19, the raiders turned back toward Saltville.

Breckenridge had left a small garrison of local troops at Saltville and had moved toward Marion to hit the back end of the raiding column. Now with less than 1,000 men at Marion, he bumped into Stoneman's force of 5,500, coming back toward Saltville. Nearly surrounded, Breckenridge was forced to go south toward North Carolina, leaving Saltville wide open.

On Dec. 20, after a daylong skirmish the Union forces pushed through the lightly defended forts on the mountains guarding Saltville. The weak home guards did not have a chance. On Dec. 21, the salt works were burned, evaporating pots broken, and cannon balls dropped down mine wells to prevent further drilling. The next day, the raiders rode back toward their bases. In just one four-day span, the targets of four years' campaigns had been taken.

The Confederates worked hard to repair the damage, and salt was being processed in a month, but the damage to the railroad hampered distribution. The lead mine repair took longer, not getting back into production until March 22, 1865, just 18 days before Lee's surrender. But the raids were not over yet. Aware of the repair efforts, Stoneman launched another raid in March 1865.

Now with the Confederacy in its dying moments, the raiders faced little opposition and proceeded to destroy every railroad engine, depot, and bridge from Bristol to Wytheville. On April 7, 1865, the lead mines were hit again. Two days later Lee surrendered at Appomattox. The lead mines had provided one-third of the 150,000,000 cartridges from the

10,000,000 pounds of lead that was produced in the Confederacy during the war. For nearly four years Yanks had tried to control the New River Valley and destroy the three strategic targets. The Confederates with only limited resources had successfully defended their strategic assets until the War was nearly over. The "minor" theater had played a key role in the course of the Civil War.

The Day Three Tour ends here at Saltville.

There are two options for returning to the start at Tamarack in Beckley, West Virginia. Both options are about the same distance, 105 miles. Option A is much quicker. Option B takes you through magnificent scenery following Burbridge's route over Clinch Mountain to Tazewell and then to I-77 and Beckley, but it goes over difficult mountain roads.

From the Salt Park turn left and drive back north on Route 91. Drive 1.4 miles back through the town of Saltville, passing the traffic light, to the intersection with Route 107.

Option A–Return–quick route. 105 miles to Tamarack. Turn right on Route 107 and return to Chilhowie. Turn left on I-81 East. Drive 33 miles past Wytheville to Exit 72. Turn to go north on I-77 toward Bluefield. Drive 71 miles north on I-77 until Tamarack.

Option B–This follows the route of General Burbridge's advance and retreat from Saltville. While this is a beautiful ride, there is a note of caution. For about five miles over Clinch Mountain the road is crushed rock/gravel. The road is in excellent condition, but is restricted to vehicles less than 35'. No one should take a camper or RV over this route.

At the intersection with Route 107 stay on Route 91 north. You will drive 34 miles to Route 460 in Tazewell. For the first 6.8 miles the road follows the North Branch of the Holston River and goes by McCready's Gap in Little Mountain. At Broadford, Route 91 turns left and begins the restricted vehicle portion. Route 42 continues straight ahead and is 38 miles to Bland, Va., and the intersection with I-77. (If you want a scenic drive without going over Clinch Mountain, drive Route 42. You continue on Route 42 all the way to Poplar Hill where it joins Route 100 – just before Cloyd's Mountain.)

On Route 91 after Broadford, the road turns to gravel in 5.6 miles. You go over the top of Clinch Mountain and the road returns to pavement after about 5 miles. Stay on Route 91 going through Liberty until the intersection with 19/460 Business Alternate. Turn left. Go 1 mile to the intersection with Route 460. Turn right on 460 and drive 28 miles to the intersection with I-77 north. Turn north on I-77 and return to Tamarack.

THE CIVIL WAR IN THE NEW RIVER VALLEY

Burbridge's Route over Clinch Mountain
Advance and Retreat • October 1864

Map 43

To Bluefield

Tazewell

Liberty

Clinch Mountain
Jefferson National Forest

Flat Top Mtn.

Broadford

Saltville

IMPORTANT
- The road over Clinch Mtn. is gravel/crushed rock.
- **NO** vehicles over two axles
- **NO** R.V.s-Campers

Acknowledgments

Author: David Bard, Ph.D., Professor of History, Concord College, Athens, WV.

Photography by Dr. David Bard unless otherwise indicated.
Photographs on pages 89, 90, 104, and 112: Tom Bone IV.
Cover Photograph by Mel Grubb.

Special thanks to Jason Brooks, who assisted in the research during the early stages of the project.

Thanks to the Civil War Workshop students who spent a summer constructing the project: Ellen Boyer, Josh Caldwell, Gayle Huffman, Fred Jones, Joanna Jones, and Tiphanie Webb.

Graphic layout: Tom Bone III and Chris Early Bone.
Maps: Tom Bone III and Fernando Porras.
Drawings and painting: Chris Early Bone.
Proofreading: Jean Beasley.

Thanks to those who assisted by test driving the routes: Bill and Helen Ryan; Jerry, Jean, and Sarah Beasley; Perry Elkins; Greg, Philip, and Kathy Ball; Mr.& Mrs. Gene Pofahl, Douglas and Carolyn Machesney, and Elizabeth K. Blatt.

Thanks to Douglas Machesney, who guided the grant and assisted in support of this project from beginning to end.

Special thanks to Carol Bard, who gave needed support and who lived "the project" for many years.

Source Notes

While the Guidebook text has not been footnoted, the author would be glad to give interested readers specific citations on request.

Below is a partial list of sources that could be investigated for further information.

General Sources:

Official Records of the War of Rebellion-Many of the quotes come from the OR.
The Virginia Regimental History Series-published by E. H. Howard-especially:
- Lowry, T. D. 22nd Virginia Infantry 1988
- Lowry, T. D. 26th Battalion Virginia Infantry 1991
- Scott, J. L. 36th Virginia Infantry 1987
- Scott, J. L. 45th Virginia Infantry 1989
- Davis, J. A. 51st Virginia Infantry 1984

West Virginia History Vol. 50-56-numerous articles.
Stutter, Boyd The Civil War in West Virginia Education Foundation, 1963
Walker, Gary The War in Southwest Virginia 1861-1865 1985

Day One Tour:

Cox, Jacob Military Reminiscences of the Civil War Scribners, 1900
Lowry, T. D. September Blood: The Battle of Carnifex Ferry Pictorial Histories, 1985
McKinney, Tim The Civil War in Fayette Co. Pictorial Histories, 1988
    Robert E. Lee and the 35th Star Pictorial Histories, 1993
    Robert E. Lee at Sewell Mountain Pictorial Histories, 1993
Williams, T. Harry Hayes of the 23rd U. Nebraska Press, 1968.

Day Two Tour:

Schmitt, Martin (ed.) General George Crook His Autobiography U. Okla. Press, 1946
Eckert, E. (ed.) Ten Years in the Saddle: Memoir of William Averell Predisio, 1978
Lowry, T. D. Last Sleep: The Battle of Droop Mountain Nov. 6, 1863 Pictorial Histories 1996

Day Three Tour:

Smith, Carlton Defend the Railroads: Battle at Giles Court House and Pigeon Roost 1995
Johnson, Patricia The United States Army Invades the New River Valley May 1864
    Printed by author, 1986
McManus, Howard The Battle of Cloyd's Mountain E. H. Howard, 1989
Marvel, The Battles for Saltville E. H. Howard, 1992

Quarrier Press
Charleston, WV

Copyright 2001 & 2004 Dr. David Bard

Funding for the original research of this book was provided by a grant from the West Virginia Humanities Council. The State of West Virginia and the West Virginia Parkways Authority were both vital in helping with the original printing of this book. Reprinted by Quarrier Press with permission.

All rights reserved. No part of this book may be reproduced in any form or means, electronic or mechanical, including photocopying recording, or by any information storage and retrieval system, without permission in writing from the publisher.

10 9 8 7 6 5 4 3 2 1

Printed in China

Library of Congress Number: 2003096900
ISBN 1-891852-34-5

The author welcomes additional information regarding the facts and depictions contained in this publication, and may be contacted at (304) 384-7601 or at Box 897, Athens, WV 24712.

Distributed by:
Pictorial Histories Distribution
1125 Central Ave.
Charleston, WV 25302
www.wvbookco.com